THE
R E L A X
FACTOR

FIVE OPEN SECRETS
TO WINNING OVER WORRY

Shannon,

Hope This Book is A
Blessing To you!

II Timothy 1:7

Dwight Henry

DWIGHT HENRY

True Potential
REACH THE WORLD

The Relax Factor
Five Open Secrets to Winning Over Worry

Cover and Interior Page design by True Potential, Inc.

ISBN: 978-1-943852-19-2 (paperback)
ISBN: 978-1-943852-20-8 (ebook)

Library of Congress Control Number: 2016934454

True Potential, Inc
PO Box 904, Travelers Rest, SC 29690
www.truepotentialmedia.com

Printed in the United States of America.

DEDICATION

To Jamie and Elliott Watson—my
incredibly gifted grandsons whom
I love so dearly. May the truth of
this book challenge and encourage
you throughout your lives.

CONTENTS

SPECIAL
APPRECIATIONS

*To Sally Askew whose advice and
assistance were invaluable
during this project.*

*To my daughters: Candi Henry and
Brittany Kylene Henry. I am so proud of
the young women you have become.*

*To my loving sisters Anne Henry and
Yvette Presswood who have stood by me
with strength and support during the hills
and valleys of my life*

*To my mother Helen Henry
and my grandmother Altha Mae
(Maudie) Brackett. The two most
influential women in my life.*

*Very special appreciation and gratitude to
Nyoka Lammie, my former wife
and mother of my daughters, for her
strength and support during
some very difficult days.*

THE RELAX FACTOR —
MY JOURNEY TO PEACE

The arrow was well into the red area, dangerously near empty. My car, as they say, was running on fumes. I was broke. In fact, I was bankrupt. I had all but surrendered in the war with depression. I'll never forget my exact location on the interstate when the Holy Spirit spoke to my heart, "I'm going to bless you like no one else in this town." I remember thinking, *Lord, I just hope I have enough gas to get home.*

FROM "WORRY WARRIOR" TO "WINNING WITNESS"

Worry is one of the most effective instruments in the devil's toolbox. Worry stifles God given creative ideas. Worry breaks up homes. Worry is linked to much of the illness in this country. Worry, left unchecked, wrecks all that is in its destructive path.

Worry never solves problems nor makes a positive difference. The "Worry Warrior" lets circumstances control him. He is not a procrastinator. He worries about tomorrow's problems today…many of which never happen.

At best, the "Worry Warrior" is just one set of circumstances away from being happy. Peace of mind is always just around the next corner. The "Worry Warrior" is destined to a life of being on the defensive and is robbed of a large part of the abundant life that Jesus offers.

AT BEST, THE "WORRY WARRIOR" IS JUST ONE SET OF CIRCUM-STANCES AWAY FROM BEING HAPPY.

Many of us have used the words "worry wart." It is appropriate that worry be likened to a wart. Just like one wart cell produces more warts to cover an entire area in short time, prolonged worry is a cover that smothers. It will damage every aspect of your life.

The "Winning Witness," on the other hand, controls circumstances. He realizes problems are a part of life. He may lose a skirmish with worry on occasion, but he always gets up and goes again. Basically, he stays on the offensive. The Winning Witness recalls past victories, which encourage him in the midst of a current challenge. Dr. Mike Murdock stated, "His mess became his message." He chooses to allow the peace of God to keep his heart and mind on Christ Jesus. His quality of life is greatly enhanced by the unchangeable and unshakable knowledge that God is vitally interested in his success in every area of life.

By no means is this the final or all-inclusive word on winning over worry. However, the biblical truths contained in **THE RELAX FACTOR** will work. Being a Winning Witness is a challenge. It is a process of learning, occasionally stumbling, correcting behavior, and growing.

Let's get started. You will **like** the trip and you will **love** the arrival.

PEACE – FOR ANYONE WHO WORRIES ABOUT ANYTHING

Talk about the bottom seemingly falling out…calamities were cascading into my life. Adverse events were happening in rapid succession. Each new day brought another train wreck. I seemed pursued by a whirlwind of disaster, which spun out of control and touched down at will in almost every area of my life.

The primary problem was business related. I owned a retail clothing enterprise, which for several months, had been failing miserably. When the economy slowed, so did my business…drastically! Each new day meant numerous calls from collection agencies and others owed money. An increasing number of creditors were filing lawsuits, resulting in embarrassing court appearances and public humiliation. Situations like these are magnified in a small town where everyone's face is familiar and the news of a failing business spreads like measles.

Bankruptcy seemed like the only alternative, and this declaration was a mammoth blow to my pride and public image. Creditors had to be notified the business was bankrupt. This was extremely painful.

AS A KNEE JERK REACTION, I WITHDREW FROM FRIENDS AND THE PUBLIC.

I had faced a number of struggles in my life, but nothing had more impact on me in terms of anxiety and depression than the collapse of this business. As a knee jerk reaction, I withdrew from friends and the public. I dreaded hearing the telephone ring. Most likely, a debt collector was calling. Seeing the mailman caused more worry and depression. Daily, he brought letters and statements of overdue accounts by the stacks. Boxes of unpaid bills accumulated. The sound of our doorbell caused fear to run through me. I did not know if a creditor, a collector, or a police officer with another lawsuit notice would greet me. Each day presented obstacles that seemed insurmountable.

In addition to my business's money problems, my personal financial situation was also deteriorating…swiftly. Two primary factors contributed to the problems. Initially, I used a great deal of personal money in an attempt to bail out the business. Secondly, my primary source of income was insurance sales. My compensation was directly tied to how much insurance I sold. Needless to say, this period of worry, concern and isolation did little to induce my enthusiasm to sell insurance. In fact, my personal sales, in which I had always taken a great deal of pride, almost bottomed out for several consecutive months. The lack of insurance sales on my part added fuel to the financial fire. Personal bills also became delinquent.

SEEING THE MAILMAN CAUSED MORE WORRY AND DEPRESSION. DAILY, HE BROUGHT LETTERS AND STATEMENTS OF OVERDUE ACCOUNTS BY THE STACKS.

Instead of picking myself up and looking at my debt as a challenge and going to work as I had always done before, I wanted to quit. I felt like yelling, "TAKE THE BUSINESS, TAKE THE HOUSE, TAKE THE CARS!

I DON'T CARE! I QUIT!" Life was miserable, but little did I know more bad news was on the way!

In the midst of this seemingly unsolvable crisis, the telephone rang one morning around 1:00 a.m. A nurse at the psychiatric hospital where my father had been a patient for over twenty years called to tell me that he was seriously ill, probably with pneumonia and other serious complications. My mother and I arrived at the hospital ninety minutes later. Daddy was barely breathing. Within two hours, he died. He was gone.

DADDY WAS BARELY BREATHING. WITHIN TWO HOURS, HE DIED. HE WAS GONE

The doctors and the chaplain came. We were ushered into a private office to begin the tedious process of notifying the family, contacting the funeral home, selecting the casket, and the numerous other details involved when a family member passes away. The funeral director, family and friends were all very comforting. However, Daddy's death seemed to push me into a deeper state of worry and depression.

Three weeks later, I sat in the same funeral home with the same director and assisted with the funeral arrangements for my step-grandfather. I had grown up respecting this man. He was a good man and a fine Christian example. His death also came as a difficult blow. The cumulative impact of all these events brought me to the point of barely being able to function.

At the office, I would sit and stare aimlessly. After snapping back to reality, I would look at the clock and realize that sometimes thirty minutes had passed. The smallest problems at work or at home completely stumped me. I had trouble wording a memo, helping with dishes, and even playing with my two-year-old daughter.

Is that when I accepted Jesus? No, I was already a Christian. I had accepted Jesus Christ as my Savior when I was thirteen years old. Was I supporting my church and honoring God with my money? Yes, the best I knew how. I had always taken an active role in our church and continued to tithe on every dollar we made even during this time of financial crisis. In fact, the material I had been teaching in our church was really coming back to perplex me. God had been dealing with me for over a year about faith, the God like faith He gives a person who has been born again (Romans 12:30). He showed me that very little takes place between Himself and a man unless faith is involved. The Bible also tells us that we are responsible for developing this faith, which God has placed in us. We also know that when this faith is fully developed in an area of our lives, then we can have what we say (Mark 11:23–24).

I started teaching these faith principles at every opportunity. Many people had never heard faith presented in that light, and they were blessed. Their obedience to God started producing results in their lives (Romans 12:3). But what about my life? Each time I taught on faith, seemingly another crack would break loose in the dam.

Herein was the true bottom line of my problem: How could I teach faith and see people change, yet I couldn't get the principles to work in my life? I was confused, not realizing I was teaching one thing and living another. My teaching was a Christian experience of good health, prosperity, and joy; my world was an increasingly emotional abyss, an unstable, crumbling financial picture, and outright depression. I was doing all I knew. Where was I missing it? Over time, this idea of not being able to live the life I was teaching brought me to a new low. My worry, my reaction, and my fear were a direct violation of the life of faith I had been describing.

Weeks went by with no relief. So utterly depressed, I completely stopped going to work. I did not want to face anything or anyone.

So now I'm on the interstate hoping I have enough gas to get home. At that exact instant I heard in my heart, "I'm going to bless you like no one else in this town." I should have listened to that still small voice, but chose instead to focus on the shrill cries of collection agents and court officers.

I made it home with little fuel to spare. There I was and there I stayed…for weeks. I barricaded myself in the bedroom with brief exits to the bathroom or kitchen. In the day, I watched television, consuming "mental candy." At night, I tossed and turned. A cloud of fear suffocated me like a blanket and robbed me of sleep like a bandit. Would these miserable merry-go-round days ever end?

> AT THAT EXACT INSTANT I HEARD IN MY HEART, "I'M GOING TO BLESS YOU LIKE NO ONE ELSE IN THIS TOWN."

My doctor, a dedicated Christian, helped me finally make the decision to seek professional help. He referred me to a Christian psychiatrist. I thought this meant immediate confinement in a hospital for an undetermined amount of time. Fear gripped me and invaded my every thought. "Here you go!" fear screamed, "You'll be in one of those places until the day you die, just like your daddy!"

It didn't exactly happen that way. For the first time in months, I heard good news! The psychiatrist thought he could treat me on an outpatient basis with prolonged regular counseling sessions. I later realized God was simply honoring the prayers of His people. A number of family and friends were interceding on my behalf. God responded to their requests, so I did not enter the hospital. I returned home!

Encouraged by not being admitted to the hospital and operating on the strength of the prayers offered on my behalf, I started talking to God like I had never talked to Him before. If I was to break the hold that worry and depression had on me, I had to rely on God and His Word.

IF I WAS TO BREAK THE HOLD THAT WORRY AND DEPRESSION HAD ON ME, I HAD TO RELY ON GOD AND HIS WORD.

I told God I still believed in His promises. I still believed that His system works. I told Him I had missed His method. I told Him I was going to find out where I missed it. At that time, I determined to get alone with God and His Word until I received what I needed to defeat the worry, anxiety, and depression that relentlessly plagued me.

I realized later I had taken the first step to victory when I told God I believed His Word was true, and I expected to have my needs met. Months before, I had wavered, wondered and even said, "I don't know if this faith thing is true or not." But when I made the fixed decision to accept the Word of God as the ultimate authority in my life, I was well on my way to winning against worry!

I got alone with God and His Word through fasting and prayer. The Holy Spirit started to deal with me almost immediately about situation and how to get out of it. I realized, as never before, God's Word has to be acted upon before results can be achieved. It is not enough to read the Word or memorize the Word, but it has to be accepted personally and acted upon in faith. In three days, I felt like a new person. God had spoken to me mightily though His Word, and I had been willing to receive and act accordingly.

> I REALIZED, AS NEVER BEFORE, GOD'S WORD HAS TO BE ACTED UPON BEFORE RESULTS CAN BE ACHIEVED.

Two weeks later, I went to an appointment with the psychiatrist. He was astounded at how rested and relaxed I was. He asked me what I had done. I told him about the steps I had taken. As a Christian psychiatrist, he smiled and said, "That's the best thing you could have done." I shook his hand, left his office, and haven't needed to go back.

God did not stop with giving me just enough of His truth to get me through that crisis. He continued guiding me in becoming a "Winning Witness." Over the next several months, I became more intensely interested in what the Word had to say about worry and how a godly man can apply those principles and concepts to his own life. After spending hours, days, weeks, months, and now years reading and meditating upon the Word of God, I am convinced God's will is for His people LIVE ABOVE WORRY OF ANY KIND!

I felt led to outline what God had given me. As the Holy Spirit directed, I began teaching these principles in area churches. I also shared the ideas on local radio. The response was heartwarming. God's Word had the same effect on those who received and acted on it as it had on me. Those who responded in faith to God's Word were set free from the mental monster that held them in captivity for many years.

God then began to guide me to put these lessons into book form—what you are holding and reading now. I haven't totally arrived, as I do not know all there is to know about winning against worry. But I continue to learn daily. I can promise your life will change dramatically if in the authority of God's Word and in the name of Jesus Christ you study these practical biblical truths about defeating worry, accept them as personal promises that belong to YOU as a child of God, and act on them regardless of how you feel or what you see.

Many Christians have remained worried and defeated their entire lives, died, and went to Heaven. Although this does happen, it's not God's best work. God wants your faith and trust in Him to grow to the point where worry is totally obliterated from your being.

It is amazing to me how we run FROM God and not TO Him in times of trouble. During my time of depression, I stopped reading the Bible for months. I saw it lying one day on the kitchen table and casually flipped the pages. They fell open on II Timothy 1:7. Verse seven leaped off the page

> GOD WANTS YOUR FAITH AND TRUST IN HIM TO GROW TO THE POINT WHERE WORRY IS TOTALLY OBLITERATED FROM YOUR BEING.

at me: "For God has not given you a spirit of fear, but of love, power and a sound mind."

Knowing the truth depends on continuing in God's Word. We can then logically conclude we will never know the truth if we don't continue in His Word. I immediately thought, *if I have such a sound mind, why do*

I feel like I'm going crazy? If a thought could be sarcastic, that one certainly qualified.

Only the truth we know will set us free. I would later realize that when you know, and you know that you know, confidence replaces fear. Back in my bedroom, which had become my cocoon, I continued to ponder that Scripture and my response. After a brief moment, something rose up in my spirit. I heard, softly but firmly, "What are you going to believe? Your feelings or My Word?" I would later realize the Holy Spirit had just asked me one of the most important questions of my life.

> I HEARD, SOFTLY BUT FIRMLY, "WHAT ARE YOU GOING TO BELIEVE? YOUR FEELINGS OR MY WORD?"

Within just over three years of being a bedroom isolationist, I was elected mayor of my city. Two years later, the people of my district sent me to the state legislature. Approximately twenty months later, I was crisscrossing the state campaigning for governor. I won my party's nomination. Eight years further down the road, God blessed me in business and I became financially successful for His purposes.

As the years passed, I often recall that still small voice I heard on the interstate when both my tank and my bank accounts were empty. "I'm going to bless you like no one else in this town." I know today as a result of God's work in me, it is this book.

The Relax Factor will impact your philosophy of life. Jeff Olson, a successful businessman and author of *The Slight Edge,* says your philosophy is what you know, and how you hold it determines how it affects your life. Your philosophy determines your attitude. Your attitude includes, in part, how you look at what you are dealing with. Adversity does not create attitude, but reveals it.

The renowned American philosopher (wink, wink) and former baseball great Yogi Berra is credited for having said, "Half the game is 90% mental." Attitude is important. Your philosophy drives your attitude. Your attitude determines habits and actions. Your habits and actions determine the quality and direction of your life.

Marriage and Christian family counselor and coach Jimmy Evans tells us "the law of the hole is to get rid of the shovel." *The Relax Factor* will teach you how to get rid of the shovel of worry and replace it with timeless, mind renewing nuggets from God's Word, which can totally reprogram your subconscious mind.

You, too, can comeback…from financial failure, from a broken relationship, from any kind of setback. With God's help there is hope and light at the end of your tunnel! But you must make some decisions about worry. Jesus has already won the war over worry. He carried our cares when He carried our sins. You can go gloriously from "Worry Warrior" to Winning Witness.

JESUS HAS ALREADY WON THE WAR OVER WORRY. HE CARRIED OUR CARES WHEN HE CARRIED OUR SINS.

I am learning it is not as important to get out of a storm, as it is to relate to the storm properly. Dr. Jimmy Arms, one of my pastors, taught us "worry is a sin … it says nobody is in control." Dr. Clarence Sexton at Temple Baptist in Knoxville, Tennessee, encourages his congregation to remember, "Our extremity is God's opportunity."

The Relax Factor is best summarized by the words of the classic hymn "Living by Faith," written by James Wells and Robert E. Winsett: *I care not today what the morrow may bring, shadows or sunshine or rain. The Lord I know ruleth o'er everything and all of my worries are vain.* The song continues:

From all harm safe in His sheltering arms, I'm living by faith and feel no alarm.

The Gospel according to John tells us, "Then Jesus said to those Jews which believed on Him, if ye continue in My word, then are ye My disciples indeed; and ye shall know the truth and the truth shall make you free" (John 8:31–32). This book is simply an exercise in continuing in God's Word as it relates to the Christian eliminating worry and replacing that worry with the principles contained in **_The Relax Factor_**.

> "WORRY IS A SIN ... IT SAYS NOBODY IS IN CONTROL." — DR. JIMMY ARMS

Pray the prayer that follows before reading any further. It is very important that this be done. It relates to God you mean business and you expect to receive His word and His promises.

Dear God, I accept your Word as the ultimate authority in my life. I believe the promises in Your Word are for me personally. I am going to apply Your Word in the areas of my life which cause me to worry. I am going to apply Your Word regardless of how I feel. I am going to apply Your Word regardless of what I see. I choose Your Word over any circumstance. I believe in my heart. I will confess with my mouth. I will not waiver. I'll have what I say. I go on re-

cord right now as having received from You a mind that is free from worry and fear. Thank You for a mind that is full of Your Love and Your Power. Thank You for the mind of Christ that is in me. In Jesus' name, Amen. (1 Corinthians 2:16)

God's plan is for us to have everything we need to live the abundant life and a future He designed for us. This includes Winning Over Worry. All His promises are ours, if we believe and receive them. As Dr. Clarence Sexton teaches, **"Your future is bright as the promises of God."**

CHAPTER 1

THE JOURNEY BEGINS

DECIDE – IT IS UP TO YOU

*D*ecide defined is "to cut from, to eliminate all other options. A decision of quality is one from which there is no retreat."

Psalm 118:24 states, "This is the day which the Lord hath made; we will rejoice and be glad in it."

As a culture, we have lulled ourselves into accepting worry as a way of life. No church member would come into a meeting bragging about a drunken binge. But worry is different, we flaunt it openly. Why? Because worry is socially and religiously accepted. In fact, it is expected! It is commonplace for tension and anxiety to completely dominate the lives of Christians. We feel we are not doing our part if we are not "worried sick" about something.

Worry is perverted faith. Worry puts faith in the problem. Worry is a product of fear. Fear is dramatically opposed to the faith by which we are saved and live. Worry is sin (Romans 14:23). God challenges His children in His Word to make some hard, fast and permanent decisions about worry. Wavering and double-mindedness closes the windows and blessings of Heaven (James 1:45).

> WORRY IS PERVERTED FAITH. WORRY PUTS FAITH IN THE PROBLEM. WORRY IS A PRODUCT OF FEAR. FEAR IS DRAMATICALLY OPPOSED TO THE FAITH BY WHICH WE ARE SAVED AND LIVE..

Are you ready for freedom-producing change? Are you ready to leap away from worry and discouragement to the life of the Bible driven principles of **The Relax Factor?** It's your decision. Dare to believe! Decide to decide! The biblical truths will work for you!

Imagine if you will, living in complete victory over worry for the rest of your life. It can happen! Ready to start the journey?

BIBLE PEACE – WHAT IT MEANS TO YOU

The word *peace* is coated with and communicates serenity. Both the Old and New Testaments are literally filled with references to Bible peace and what it can accomplish in the life of the believer.

The Prophet Isaiah wrote of the coming of the Prince of Peace (Isaiah 9:6). Isaiah said, "Of the increase of His government and peace there will be no end..." (Isaiah 9:7). He also wrote whoever focused or kept his thoughts on Christ would be kept in perfect peace (Isaiah 26:3). Isaiah 26:12 declares, "Lord, Thou will ordain peace for us, for thou also hath wrought all our works in us." The prophet states, "The work (end result) of righteousness shall be peace." The Hebrew word for *peace* used in these scriptural contexts means "health, prosperity, favor and rest." Another definition is "safe in mind and body."

Think about the scope of these Hebrew words for peace. Now let us consider Isaiah 26:3: "Thou wilt keep him in perfect peace, whose mind is stayed on Thee; because he trusteth in Thee." Without violating the Scripture, we could substitute "health, prosperity, favor and rest" for the word *peace*. Thou will keep him in perfect health. Thou will keep him in perfect prosperity. Thou will keep him in perfect favor. Thou will keep him in perfect rest. Thou will keep him safe in mind and body. As was once said, "If this doesn't light your fire, your wood is definitely wet!"

Our key to victory in Isaiah 26:3 is keeping our mind "stayed" on the Lord. The Hebrew word for *stayed* in this text is "chamak" (sawmak). Translated it means "to lie hard, lean upon, to take hold, to rest self, or to sustain." Again, the secret to the promise is to STAY not PLAY. As believers, we have the tendency to PLAY with a promise for a while. Then, like a child, bored with one toy and wanting another, we move on. Our job is to keep our mind "stayed" (fixated). God's job is to "keep" us in perfect peace.

There is more to the definition of the word *peace* as used in Isaiah. It means "to be complete, to be made whole, to be restored and to be paid back." God says, if we keep our minds stayed on Him, then we can get back whatever has been taken from us…our health, our money, our emotional stability, our purpose or direction in life. *Peace* is often said to mean "nothing missing, nothing broken." Wait! There's still more! The word *shalom* which Isaiah uses on many occasions, means to be "fitted or made ready." Buckle your seatbelts! This is going to be a great ride!

God is your creator, your manufacturer. He knows you inside and out. He already knows every problem and challenge you will have in your lifetime. He knows what kind of peace you will need and when you will need it. God has a plan of peace "fitted, made ready," or customized to meet your unique and personal needs. It is tailor made with only you in mind. God loves us all enough to design a plan of peace just for us! Our job again…keep our minds "stayed" on Him, and let Him clothe us with His perfectly and uniquely designed plan of peace.

> GOD SAYS, IF WE KEEP OUR MINDS STAYED ON HIM, THEN WE CAN GET BACK WHATEVER HAS BEEN TAKEN FROM US…

Isaiah 26:12 gives us more insight into the God kind of peace: "Lord, Thou wilt ordain peace for us: for Thou also hast wrought all our works in us." Further study of this verse tells us the Lord will ordain peace for them who keep their minds stayed on Him. There is a major blessing in the word *ordain* (establish). It simply means "to make arrangement for." Think about a family vacation. Think about making all the arrangements. Think about someone to check your mail, watch your house and take care of your pets. Think about purchasing all those extra vacation items, about packing, getting your vehicle serviced and contacting the appropriate friends and family members to let them know where to reach you. The list goes on.

It would be much easier just to get in the car and go without making all the arrangements. In like fashion, we often attempt to take control in making the arrangements for our own peace of mind. God simply says to keep your mind on Him and His Word. He has made all the arrangements for your peace. He's working everything out! God is always working for our good! (Deuteronomy 6:24) The New Testament is full of promises of the power of peace in our lives. Notice the priority Jesus gives supernatural peace. His dying legacy to the church is recorded in John 14:27: "Peace I leave with you, My peace I give unto you..." What does that mean? The word for *peace* used here means "to join, to set at one again, a divine influence upon the heart." In other words, Jesus is saying, "I've joined you back to God, you and the Father are together again. Your very nature can be influenced and changed." Now that's real Bible peace!

CHRIST HAS DONE ALL THAT IS NECESSARY FOR YOU TO HAVE COMPLETE PEACE. IT'S YOUR MOVE!

In that light, Paul boldly wrote to the church at Rome that to be spiritually minded was life and peace (Romans 8:6). A mind set to obey our newly created spirit (or heart) will produce peace of heart, soul and body. As it has been said, when our heart works right, our head will work right as well. In fact, Paul told the Corinthians "God has called us to peace." You may or may not have a call as a pastor, teacher or evangelist, but every Christian has a "Call to Peace!" Will you answer the call? Christ extended this invitation just like all the other benefits of salvation. Christ has done all that is necessary for you to have complete peace. It's your move!

Note Paul's desire for the New Testament churches when he writes:

Romans 1:7 "…Grace to you and peace from God our Father, and the Lord Jesus Christ"

I Corinthians 1:3 "Grace be unto you, and peace…"

II Corinthians 1:2 "Grace be to you and peace…"

Galatians 1:3 "Grace be to you and peace …"

Ephesians 1:2 "Grace be to you and peace from God our Father and from the Lord Jesus Christ."

Philippians 1:2 "Grace be unto you, and peace…"

Colossians 1:2 "…Grace be unto you, and peace…"

I Thessalonians 1:1 "Grace be unto you, and peace…"

II Thessalonians 1:2 "Grace unto you, and peace..."

Titus 1:4 "...grace, mercy and peace from God the Father and the Lord Jesus Christ..."

Philemon 1:3 "Grace to you, and peace..."

Observe Peter's greetings in his letters. In both I Peter 1:2 and II Peter 1:2, he says, "Grace unto you and peace be multiplied."

Notice John's exhortation to the body of Christ in III John verse, 14 "...Peace be unto thee..."

Jude greets the believers in Christ in verse 2, "Mercy unto you and peace and love be multiplied."

Do you think the Holy Spirit is trying to tell us something about peace? I think so!

A central truth communicated in the Scriptures is that our peace can be broadened. It can grow and cover those areas of our life that were previously ruled by fear and worry. The prayer is that believers in Christ be filled with God's supernatural force of peace. If this were not possible, Paul would not have prayed for it. Peter would not have proclaimed it. John would not have emphasized it, and Jude would not have spotlighted it. Peace is for you. Will you be for peace...or for worry?

CHAPTER 2

RECEIVE YOUR SOUND MIND

I have often heard people share they need to receive something from God's Word and the Bible seems to fall open to the very verse they needed. This was a first time experience for me. It has not happened since. God knew I needed something quick and powerful to solve the immediate crisis in my life. He also knew I needed some instruction in His Word to give me the power with Him as the constant resource to keep the crisis from ever occurring again. He provided both.

"Wherefore I put thee in remembrance that thou stir the gift of God, which is in thee by the putting on of my hands. For God hath not given us the spirit of fear; but of power, and of love, and of a sound mind." (II Timothy 1:6–7)

Examine closely what Paul was saying to Timothy. First, he said you must stir up the gift that is within you. What Gift? The gift of love, power and a sound mind. Paul compares this to a fire, which must be stirred up and have more fuel added, else the force of its flames and heat will diminish. First, let us consider the gift, then the issue of stirring it up.

Did you know God has given you a spirit of love, power and a sound mind? What is a sound mind exactly? The word *sound* comes from the Greek "sophroniza," which means "to discipline or correct." In other words, your mind can be disciplined, corrected and brought under control. You do not have to be a puppet of emotions, worry, or fear. *The Relax Factor* will walk you further into the practical applications of this wonderful gift…a mind that can be renewed!

YES, IN SPITE OF THE WORRY AND ANXIETY YOU MAY BE FEELING RIGHT NOW, GOD HAS EQUIPPED YOU WITH A SOUND MIND.

Yes, in spite of the worry and anxiety you may be feeling right now, God has equipped you with a sound mind. How many times have we chosen not to use the equipment God has given us? That is the case when Paul writes there is a spirit of fear, but it is not of God. We can then conclude this spirit of fear and worry is from Satan. This spirit of fear is one of the devil's primary tools in preventing Christians from living a victorious, worry free life. We learn in the Gospel according to Mark 4:19, "the cares of this world" choke the Word of God in our life. However, let us not forget the "sound mind" God has given the believer. Let's unpack some of the tools that God has given us to bring our mind under control.

> THIS SPIRIT OF FEAR IS ONE OF THE DEVIL'S PRIMARY TOOLS IN PREVENTING CHRISTIANS FROM LIVING A VICTORIOUS, WORRY FREE LIFE.

II Timothy 1:7 points out that in addition to a sound mind, we have been given love and power. When I read this verse in my earlier described mentally depressed state, my first reactions was, "But I don't feel like I have a sound mind." It was as if God pricked my spirit and said, "Your feelings have nothing to do with it. Are you going to believe your feelings or My Word?" I knew what He was saying. I was at a very important crossroads in my life. Was I going to accept my feelings as the ultimate authority or His Word? The correct choice was obvious. Since God's Word says He had given me a sound mind, then I had a sound mind, a mind that could be reprogrammed and remodeled. So right then and there, I began to praise God for my sound mind, even though I didn't feel it was.

I began to say, "Thank You, Father, for my sound mind. Thank you it is Your gift to me. Thank You it is greater than the spirit of fear. I received my sound mind and will start to put it into operation in my life. Devil, you will have to take your spirit of fear and leave!" I had to accept my sound mind just like I had received my salvation…by faith. Sure, Satan tried again many times after that day to put the same worry and fear in me again. I have the power to tell Satan, "No, Satan. I refuse to accept the spirit of fear. God has given me a sound mind, and the spirit of fear cannot penetrate the sound mind God has given me." I have the mental ability to choose strength over Satan. Then I would praise God again.

My attitude began to noticeably change. Before learning the truth about what God had given me, depression met me the very second I opened my eyes every morning and stayed with me all day. After learning the truth about my sound mind, I started speaking the Word of God to the spirit of fear when it tried to creep in to control me. I resisted it primarily using II Timothy 1:7. The Bible says to resist the devil, and he will flee from you. I discovered that to be true with the spirit of fear. The more of God's Word I spoke, the less the spirit of fear bothered me. In just a few days, I caught myself waking up and looking forward to facing the day. What a change! What a miracle!

The key was to stop the spirit of fear the second it attempted to control my mind. It was much more difficult to stop it after even only 15–20 seconds of worry. It has to be halted at once, with the Word of God. It will obey God's Word every time. It will flee and be less and less of a problem for you, as long as you continue to make God's Word the ultimate authority in your life.

Learning this one truth regarding my sound mind began to free me from the bondage of worry and

> THE KEY WAS TO STOP THE SPIRIT OF FEAR THE SECOND IT ATTEMPTED TO CONTROL MY MIND.

move me toward becoming a "Winning Witness." It will work for you, too. God's system is perfect, and He is no respecter of persons (Acts 10:34, KJV)—He won't discriminate or show favoritism among His people. Regardless of how you feel or what you see, begin to believe in your heart and confess with your mouth God has given you a sound mind. James 4:7 says, "Therefore submit to God. Resist the devil and he will flee from you." Praise God for that gift! *You will find practical "How Tos" for training and remodeling your mind in Chapter 3 – Realize the Effect of Worry.*

God had not finished dealing with me about being a Christian and struggling with worry. He had shown me the dynamic truth to help me overcome the raging crisis in my life. After the fire was extinguished, he led me into His Word and helped me to see, as never before, that He wanted His children to be worry free.

Notice I did not say, "problem free." God does not transport us to a spiritual "never, never land." Problems will continue to come. In fact, buckle you seatbelts because the more of the Word of God that abides in you, the bigger the "fiery darts" of the devil will be. However, in spite of the efforts of the spirit of fear, in spite of the efforts of the devil, it is possible as a child of God to live

> IN SPITE OF THE EFFORTS OF THE DEVIL, IT IS POSSIBLE AS A CHILD OF GOD TO LIVE TOTALLY ABOVE WORRY.

totally above worry. I believe without reservation that as you continue to read, God's wisdom, which is available to every believer (James 4:17), will begin to operate in your spirit. I believe you are on your way to being set free from the bondage of the spirit of fear. I believe the eyes of your understanding about winning over worry are about to open as never before. I believe God will use **_The Relax Factor_** to take your trust in Him to a higher level.

RELAX YOUR BEING

The following five chapters outline practical life changing steps for extinguishing worry and allowing God's peace to rule in your life. I've also developed five ideas to encourage you **to Relax**:

R realize worry's effect and remodel your mind

E exercise faith

L look to the Word

A always cast your care

X "xercise" patience

When tempted to worry, remember … **Relax!**

CHAPTER 3

REALIZE THE EFFECTS OF WORRY AND REMODEL YOUR MIND

REMODEL YOUR MIND

A song from the classic production of *The Sound of Music* reminds us *Let's start at the beginning … a very good place to start.* The very beginning of learning **The Relax Factor** is mental housecleaning and remodeling. Simply stated, the mind **must** be reprogrammed.

It is no secret Satan first and foremost wants to control our mind to keep us from Christ. The devil wants us to take *his* thoughts, think about them until they become *our* thoughts, speak them and then act on them. If Satan controls our mind, he controls our life. God made us so our subconscious mind receives all information as fact. Whatever message it constantly receives, it will work to bring that information into physical reality.

Winning over worry starts with "house cleaning" our thought life. Tearing down old thought patterns where worry has been allowed to roam is the first order of the day. Romans 12:2 says, "And be not conformed to this world: but be ye transformed by the renewing of your mind, that ye may prove what is that good, and acceptable, and perfect, will of God."

WINNING OVER WORRY STARTS WITH "HOUSE CLEANING" OUR THOUGHT LIFE.

In II Corinthians 10:5 we read, "Casting down imaginations, and every high thing that exalteth itself against the knowledge of God, and bringing into captivity thought to the obedience of Christ." When a thought of worry or fear pops into my head, I say, "Hey, you alien and trespassing thought, get out of my mind in Jesus' name." Then I begin to praise God for my sound mind.

In addition to mental house cleaning, students of *The Relax Factor* renew their mind with the "right stuff." Paul's letter to the Romans 10:17 states emphatically "...faith cometh by hearing..." In the original Greek, *hearing* is tied to the audience. In other words, what we give audience or pay attention to is where we develop faith. What we take in is what we act out. On what we focus or pay attention to is what we become. Romans 12:22 challenges us not to be conformed to this world but be transformed by the renewing of our mind. Winning Witnesses are not conformed to this world's system or way of doing things. The world worries and frets. The Winning Witness is renewing or remodeling his mind with God's promises, which build faith.

> THE WINNING WITNESS IS ALSO VERY SELECTIVE ABOUT THE "THOUGHTS" HE ENTERTAINS.

The Winning Witness is also very selective about the "thoughts" he entertains. Matthew 6:25 and Luke 11:25 tell us we do not have to accept every thought we get. The Winning Witness does not meditate on negative thoughts and does not give them life by continuing to speak them.

The Psalms teach us God's mind is full of us, not the heavens, not the moon, nor the stars, but US the beings created in His image…mankind. One day I heard myself praying, "God, I want my mind to be as full of You as Your mind is full of me." ***The Relax Factor*** is my story of that journey. Remodeling the mind is an absolute essential process in order to move forward on this trip. Psalm 8:4a says, "What is man that You are mindful of him?"

What is unique about worry? Why is it many Christians who would not consistently and consciously be involved in anything that contradicts God's Word not only practice worry but often also wear it as a badge of honor?

Suppose a member of your family is having serious physical problems. The situation appears to be worsening. Everyone around you expresses deep concern and fear. Someone approaches you and states, "I know you must be very worried." You immediately respond, "No, not at all." Can you imagine the reaction of those around you? "What do you mean, 'not at all'?" the person asks. At that point, even the love for your family member may come into question. You may not even be given time to say you turned over that care to God. The Bible says we can be carefree (I Peter 5:7).

Regardless of any situation, you are to walk in victory and above worry. This is not to say you should hold things in and never mention your problems and needs to you brothers and sisters in the Lord. However, once you have offered prayer and released faith, start acting and speaking like you believe what you prayed.

THE EFFECTS OF WORRY

So what are the bottom-line effects of worry?

WORRY VIOLATES GOD'S WORD

Make no mistake about the fact that worry on the part of the believer violates God's Word. Remember the children of Israel and their trip from Egypt to Canaan? On numerous occasions when a need would arise, they seemingly blotted out all the great miracles God had performed in their midst. Instantly and in almost complete unity, they would begin lamenting, "It would have been better to have stayed in Egypt than to die here in the wilderness." Time after time, God met their needs. He provided them with protection from Pharaoh's army and with food, water, and direction day and night, not to mention their actual great escape from Egypt. However, they allowed worry and the spirit of fear to control them, even as they were on the threshold of the Promised Land.

All they could talk about was dying in the wilderness. You know what happened? They got what they spoke. They died in the wilderness. Joshua and Caleb were the only two members of that generation who made it into "the land of milk and honey." Joshua and Caleb had a choice...worry or stand in faith.

> THE VERY APPEARANCE OF ANOTHER CRISIS OFTEN SEEMS TO PUSH SOME OF US AUTOMATICALLY INTO A STATE OF ANXIETY AND CONCERN.

The masses chose to worry. Joshua and Caleb chose to stand in faith. The worriers died. Joshua and Caleb led the next generation of Israelites to great victories in Canaan. Does the story of the children of Israel sound like anyone you know? Examine your own life. Recall the many past times when God has moved mightily to solve a problem for you. Yet the very appearance of another crisis often seems to push some of us automatically into a state of anxiety and concern, like the children of Israel. We seem to dismiss from our minds the numerous occasions God has miraculously pulled us through. We react in fear, and not in faith (Hebrews 6:11).

WORRY LIMITS GOD'S WORK IN YOUR LIFE

James, the half brother of Jesus, had some stern statements about the person who allows worry to rule any aspect of his life. He wrote, "But let him ask in faith, nothing wavering. For he that wavereth is like a wave of the sea driven with the wind and tossed. For let not that man think that he shall receive anything of the Lord. A double-minded man is unstable in all his ways" (James 1:6–8).

Examine these verses in detail. James tells us to ask of God in faith. The worried person is not asking in faith. He bounces back and forth by circumstances and situations much like water is tossed and driven by the wind. This is a vivid picture of complete instability. This person is a puppet whose strings are pulled by whatever events and feelings are present that day.

> WE SEEM TO DISMISS FROM OUR MINDS THE NUMEROUS OCCASIONS GOD HAS MIRACULOUSLY PULLED US THROUGH.

Sarah Young, in her wonderful book of devotions, ***Jesus Calling,*** *Enjoying Peace in His Presence,* addresses the matter of feelings from a Bible-based perspective. She writes, "Feelings per se are not sinful, but they can be temptations to sin. Affirm your trust in God regardless of how you feel. If you persist, your feelings will eventually fall in line with your faith."

Young also encourages the Christ follower not to "hide from fear or pretend it isn't there. Anxiety that you hide in the recesses of your heart will give birth to fear of fear: a monstrous stepchild." Bring your anxieties into the light of God's presence, where you can deal with them together. Young concludes, as God would instruct the believer, "concentrate on trusting Me, and fearfulness will gradually lose its foothold within you."

BRING YOUR ANXIETIES INTO THE LIGHT OF GOD'S PRESENCE, WHERE YOU CAN DEAL WITH THEM TOGETHER.

For now, know this: God is a gentleman. He does not force Himself on us when we accept salvation, nor will He force Himself on us in terms of snatching away our problems in spite of our own will. You remain, even after becoming a Christian, a free moral agent with choices and decisions to make. When you choose worry instead of giving a problem to God, without wavering, then you have limited God to take ultimate and complete control of that problem because it would override your will. God will not do that.

WORRY IS A SIN

Remember: the choice is yours…the peace of God or worry. Start now to choose God's promise every time. There can be no doubt that worry in our life is sin. Paul told the church at Rome, "But he who doubts is condemned if he eats, because he does not eat from faith, for whatsoever is not from faith is sin (Romans 14:23)."

F. J. Dake comments on this verse in *Dake's Annotated Reference Bible.* He makes such a powerful statement that it needs to be registered and stored in our spirit. Dake maintains that the sin mentioned in the verse refers to "Anything done to violate the faith principle by which one is saved and by which he lives."

> REMEMBER: THE CHOICE IS YOURS…THE PEACE OF GOD OR WORRY.

Worry certainly violates that principle. Since worry within the life of the believer is sin, the believer should confess and repent to God. Worry should not be condoned or flaunted in the life of a Christian any more than any other sin. However, God is merciful. He will forgive you and cleanse you from all unrighteousness. You only need to ask!

Worry removes God from His proper place. When worry has prominence over the promises of God, worry becomes an idol (James 1:6).

> WORRY REMOVES GOD FROM HIS PROPER PLACE. WHEN WORRY HAS PROMINENCE OVER THE PROMISES OF GOD, WORRY BECOMES AN IDOL (JAMES 1:6).

Choosing worry removes God from authority. As Joshua challenged the children of Israel, "Choose this day whom you will serve." Worry and fear is a choice. When one chooses worry and fear over the person and promises of God, the need or circumstance becomes an idol. God is essentially removed from His place of prominence, only to be replaced by the spirit of fear. It happens by choice when we choose worry over God.

A former pastor of mine often proclaimed "nothing is dynamic until it's specific." Therein lies an answer. The key is deciding to make God's Word specific regarding the situation which brings pressure and worry into your life. Return the pressure to the problem with intensity, over whatever period of time necessary, and launch an attack of the Word of God on the issue at hand.

WORRY NEVER EVER, EVER HELPS

Worry and anxiety simply add nothing positive to any moment or situation.

Jesus taught His disciples this lesson. It is recorded in Luke 12. Keep in mind these were men who walked with Jesus daily. Worry was a problem for them.

Jesus said take no thought about the needs of life. The lesson was just because a "worry" thought comes our way, we don't have to take it. We don't have to keep it in our mind. We don't have to give it more life by continuing to speak it from our mouth. Jesus emphasized taking in no thoughts of worry or fear because they produce anxiety only. It will not add "one cubit to our

> JUST BECAUSE A "WORRY" THOUGHT COMES OUR WAY, WE DON'T HAVE TO TAKE IT. WE DON'T HAVE TO KEEP IT IN OUR MIND.

stature." A cubit is 18 inches; stature refers to height or growth. In other words, Jesus said worry never moves us forward, solves our problems, or adds anything uplifting to our lives. In fact, worry will separate us from the very promises of God that will bring peace and joy to our lives.

Paul writes in the Book of Romans (6:23), "For the wages of sin is death; but the gift of God is eternal life through Jesus Christ our Lord." *Wages of sin* is the payday for continuing to miss the mark. *Death* is the separation from God in that context. *Gift of God* is self-explanatory. *Eternal life* begins the instant we accept the work of Christ personally and invite Him into our life.

> WORRY WILL SEPARATE US FROM THE VERY PROMISES OF GOD THAT WILL BRING PEACE AND JOY TO OUR LIVES.

Romans 6:23 is not limited to the time after we leave this earth and spend eternity with God in Heaven or the time after we are separated from Him in hell. Romans 6:23 is a here and now verse.

In choosing to remain on the "sin" path of worry, we separate ourselves from God as it relates to a particular need or problem; thus, we allow the cares of this world to make His Word unfruitful (Matthew 13:22). Yes, Christ followers who worry a lot die and go to Heaven every day. However, that crowd misses God's best... having an abundant life now. One definition of the Greek word *abundant* is "advantage beyond measure." Remember: worry never ever, ever helps!

WORRY ERODES GOD'S BEST

One definition of the word *worry* is "to strangle." A wolf is said to worry (or strangle) a sheep. Worry can't strangle the Word of God, but it can make it unfruitful in the life of a person who chooses to focus on the problem instead of the promises of God (Matthew 13:22, Mark 4:19).

Imagine that...the Word that contains God's life and breath can be choked by choice. When we choose worry over the ultimate truth, God's promises can be choked

WHEN WE CHOOSE WORRY OVER THE ULTIMATE TRUTH, GOD'S PROMISES CAN BE CHOKED TO THE POINT OF BEING UNPRO-DUCTIVE IN OUR LIFE OR ISSUE.

to the point of being unproductive in our life or issue. If believers really understood the damage worry causes, we'd all avoid it like the plague.

WORRY EXTINGUISHES HOPE

The word *hope* is used in the Bible more than 120 times. *Hope* is essentially "a mental picture of the future." God's kind of hope produces a mental picture of the future as one of confident expectation. Worry attacks this confident expectation. We learn in Proverbs 13:12: "Hope deferred makes the heart sick." In other words, confident expectation postponed makes your heart sick. When your heart is sick, your mental image changes and when the mental image changes, often times you are hindered from going into the future God has planned for you. Worry is often subtle but always a spiritual weapon of mass destruction. It puts the brakes on and prohibits believers from walking into all that God has planned for them.

WORRY ANNIHILATES THE BODY

The act of redemption that Jesus provided with His death, burial and resurrection addresses all three parts of our being: spirit, soul and body. Jesus' mission was to bring "peace" between the Father and the human race, to meet needs, and bring harmony to our complete being.

Just as Jesus blessed us in spirit, soul and body, worry attacks all parts of the epitome of God's creation. Worry robs us of the joy of our re-created spirit, replaces peace of mind (soul) with fear, and annihilates the temple of the Holy Spirit…the body.

The following is a portion of an article appearing on the website Healthy-Lifestyle.most-effective-solution.com:

> WORRY IS OFTEN SUBTLE BUT ALWAYS A SPIRITUAL WEAPON OF MASS DESTRUCTION.

Worrying can have a gross negative impact on our body, which can lead to physical illness. Worrying incessantly can cast a pall of gloom on everything you do. It can negatively impact your appetite, relationships, activity, lifestyle habits, sleep and job performance.

It also states:

Continuous worrying, emotional stress, too much of anxiety – all of these can have a heavy toll on your physical health. Stress and anxiety caused by too much worrying acts as the trigger for the body to get into a fight or flight mode, as a result of which, the body's sympathetic nervous system releases stress hormones like cortisol into the body's system. These hormones cause blood sugar level and triglycerides i.e. the blood fats to rise significantly, in preparation for the body to use as fuel. However, if such changes taking place in the body occurs on a regular basis, problems begin to crop up. The presence of these hormones in the system leads to several physical reactions such as:

Difficulty in swallowing	Muscle tension
Dizziness	Nausea
Dryness in the mouth	Nervous energy
Rapid heartbeat	Rapid breathing
Fatigue	Shortness of breath
Problem in concentrating	Sweating profusely
Irritability	Trembling and twitching
Muscle pain	Headache

However, if the body does not perform active physical activity to utilize the excessive fuel that has entered the blood stream, it can lead to serious consequences in physical health. These include:

Muscle tension	Digestive problems
Short-term memory loss	Heart attack
Premature coronary artery disease	Suppression of the natural immune system

If proper treatment is not meted out in cases of high anxiety or stress, depression sets in. In extreme cases, it can even give rise to suicidal thoughts. Also, what has to be understood thoroughly is these effects are what you are prone to be affected with in cases of severe stress. For that, stress is merely the trigger. It all depends on how well we are able to cope with stressful situations. Stress does not make us ill. Instead it is the after effects of stress like excessive anxiety or tension that has a damaging effect on our body, causing physical illness.

Research indicates worrying adversely affects your heart and can bring about heart disease. It also adversely affects your immune, digestive, nervous and reproductive systems.

Worry and anxiety are no small matters, stealing from their victims both quality and quantity of life. Do you remember why Satan came? According to John 10:10, "to kill, steal and destroy."

> IF PROPER TREATMENT IS NOT METED OUT IN CASES OF HIGH ANXIETY OR STRESS, DEPRESSION SETS IN. IN EXTREME CASES, IT CAN EVEN GIVE RISE TO SUICIDAL THOUGHTS.

REMODELING – THE ROOT OF REWARD

The Apostle Paul – God's human penman for the book of Romans (12:2) offers life-changing instruction: "… be ye not conformed to this world, but be ye transformed by the renewing of your mind." A word-by-word analysis of this verse provides better understanding of its significance:

UNTIL YOU MAKE IT SPECIFIC TO YOU, IT'S JUST INFORMATION WITHOUT REVELATION.

Ye…until you make it specific to you, it's just information without revelation.

Not…the Greek for *not* is defined as not. What it is about *not* that we do not understand.

Conformed…means a pattern or mold

World…the world's way of doing or being

Transformed…the Greek word is *metamorphoo,* from which we get metamorphosis. A word which is often used to describe the caterpillar to butterfly process.

Renewing is a way to refer to remodeling. Remodeling defines the process of getting old "stuff" out and new "stuff" in. "Stuff" being everything you take in and believe.

Thus Paul is saying don't get into the world's pattern or mold for doing or being, but be changed completely by the remodeling of your mind with new material. As we know, our spirits are changed completely when we receive Christ. We become what the Bible calls "new creatures" (II Corinthians 5:17).

Our minds, however, must be continually renewed or remodeled. The new material must be the Word of God. The Word of God must be our final authority and our constant point of reference.

> DON'T GET INTO THE WORLD'S PATTERN OR MOLD FOR DOING OR BEING, BUT BE CHANGED COMPLETELY BY THE REMODELING OF YOUR MIND WITH NEW MATERIAL.

Everything and everyone else changes, but God's Word will never pass away. (Matthew 24:35, Mark 13:31) Situations may arise in our lives that are tragic, harmful or create real needs…real facts can tempt us to worry. God's truth can change facts.

Only if we continue in His Word will we know the truth, and the truth will set us free (John 8:32). **Remodeling our mind with the Word of God is the root of reward.**

Before reading any further, stop now and begin to talk to God about the worry in your life. Tell God you recognize your worry is displeasing to Him. Tell Him you realize your worry limits Him. Go on record before God now as sincerely desiring to defeat worry. Ask God to make you fertile ground to receive His Word. Tell Him that as you receive, you will act on it in full.

> STOP NOW AND BEGIN TO TALK TO GOD ABOUT THE WORRY IN YOUR LIFE. GO ON RECORD BEFORE GOD NOW AS SINCERELY DESIRING TO DEFEAT WORRY.

As you continue to learn from the truth about worry, then the truth will set you free. Thank God for the liberty we have in His Word.

CHAPTER 4

EXERCISE FAITH

When facing a problem, we have been told, "You've got to have faith." That is true, but first you must have God. Our goal is God, almost everything else is a by product. We find faith **described** in Hebrews 11:1 as "Now faith is the substance of things hoped for, the evidence of things not seen." We find faith **defined** also in the Book of Hebrews 12:2 as "…looking unto Jesus the author and finisher of our faith…" The definition of *faith* is "looking unto Jesus." Remember the goal is always God. If we know God, we will know faith as well as love, joy, peace, grace, etc.

Let us examine faith. What is it? Where do you get it? How do you make it work in your life? What is the God kind of faith? To be sure, it is more than just a positive outlook. Those who operate in true God given faith have positive attitudes; however, the God kind of faith goes deeper than that.

The God kind of faith is a force. It is a power. It originates in God Himself. God uses this faith to render helpless Satan's spirit of fear. The faith inside of God does not doubt, worry, or fear. When God uses His faith to "frame the worlds" (Hebrews 11:3), He at no time doubted the world would be created. He spoke, He expected it to be, and the world was created.

THE GOD KIND OF FAITH IS A FORCE. IT IS A POWER. IT ORIGINATES IN GOD HIMSELF.

When God was about to create light, He did not say, "I don't know if this will work or not." No, He said, while operating in faith, "Let there be light" (Genesis 1:3). What happened? There was light! His faith was "the substance of things hoped for, the evidence of things not seen" (Hebrews 11:1). He hoped for "the worlds." He spoke His faith, and His faith gave substance to the worlds. Yes, the worlds were framed by His faith.

Faith still works exactly like that today if developed properly and exercised according to the instructions of the Bible. It will add substance as well and bring into being those things we cannot yet see. Your faith can bring your healing into being, your money into being, not to mention, your salvation into being.

There are other biblical examples of God using His faith. His raising Jesus from the dead is a miraculous illustration; however, in summary, Bible faith is a force that resides in the very being of God.

> YOUR FAITH CAN BRING YOUR HEALING INTO BEING, YOUR MONEY INTO BEING, NOT TO MENTION, YOUR SALVATION INTO BEING.

Where does the Christian get faith? The Apostle Paul did a beautiful job of relating what God places in the spirit of the person who is born again: "But the fruit of the Spirit is love, joy, peace, longsuffering, gentleness, goodness, faithfulness, gentleness, self-control. Against such there is no law" (Galatians 5:22–23).

Try to understand the full impact of what happened when Jesus comes into our lives. Receiving Christ personally is much more than a decision that allows one to escape an eternity in hell. Our eternal life started when we are born again. There is no need to put off until Heaven some of the great blessings and benefits that are available to us now. Jesus comes to dwell in you when you become a Christian. "Do you not know that you are the temple of God and that the Spirit of God dwells in you?" (I Corinthians 3:16)

God also placed inside His children a number of Godlike qualities, graces, if you will, that are available for your growth, benefit, pleasure and His glory. Those are the qualities and the powers to which Paul referred in Galatians 5:22–23. All Christians have all of them residing in their spirit. God put them there when we accepted Christ, and why should He not? After all, you became a member of His family, a joint heir with Jesus Christ Himself (Romans 8:17). If Jesus had these forces operating in Him, and you are a joint heir with Him, then it is only reasonable that you have them, too.

> GOD ALSO PLACED INSIDE HIS CHILDREN A NUMBER OF GODLIKE QUALITIES, GRACES, IF YOU WILL, THAT ARE AVAILABLE FOR YOUR GROWTH, BENEFIT, PLEASURE AND HIS GLORY.

Primarily, we are dealing with the force of faith in our life. However, as we are transformed more and more into the image of Christ, all nine graces of the Fruit of the Spirit will be operating. How can this happen? It happens when you are diligent with the Word of God. Learn all you can about the Fruit of the Spirit. Exactly what is meant by "longsuffering, meekness, temperance," etc.? Then when you realize the Fruit of the Spirit was placed by God inside you, and you have learned from the Bible about each part of the single fruit, you will discover that various, and eventually all, parts of the fruit will become evident in your life.

Faith is the part of the fruit that needs to be explored here. Because, in terms of implementing the principles in **The Relax Factor,** there can be no doubt your God given faith is of tremendous importance in defeating the spirit of fear. As already discussed, faith lives inside each child of God. Additionally, God gives every Christian the same amount of the same type of faith. "…God hath dealt to each one a measure of faith" (Romans 12:3).

If then faith is used as a primary force in relaxing, then it stands to reason the stronger our faith is the less problem worry becomes. That conclusion logically leads to the third question posed about our faith. How do you put it to work effectively? The measure of faith must be strong. To be strong, like the body, faith needs to be fed and exercised. How is faith fed, and why is it important to constantly feed it? The Bible tells us "…faith comes by hearing, and hearing by the Word of God" (Romans 10:17). *Hearing* is defined as "to give audience to." A good audience member is totally involved in the performance. The action on the stage has his total attention. He feels almost as if he is part of that action. So it is as well with the Word of God. True hearing means you're not only going through the Word, but the Word is also going through you. It becomes a part of you. It is written on your heart. The Word becomes personal…a "rhema" word poured into you. A rhema word is one that reveals truth, and truth sets you free. In this case, free from the care of the issue pressing you. When that kind of hearing happens, faith comes. Simply stated, faith feeds on the Word. If the faith God has given us is continually fed the Word of God, then more faith will come.

Faith comes from listening to and obeying God. How else does faith work…by praying…no; by fasting… no; by giving…no. Praying, fasting and giving are certainly essential acts of spiritual growth and contribute to faith, but faith comes only from the hearing of the Word of God. Understand this, hearing the Word goes much deeper than just having it pass through your ears. Hearing means receiving and obeying. Hearing means allowing the Word to abide in or become a part of you. That is why Jesus tells us, "If you abide in me, and my words abide in you, you shall ask what you will, and it shall be done unto you" (John 15:7). I once heard a teacher say the Bible is "the factory for your faith."

Yes, if your faith is going to be great, a faith that overcomes and defeats worry, then it must be fed a substantial and steady diet of the Word of God. If it means adjusting your schedule and lifestyle in order to make time for the Word of God, then by all means adjust. You must get very personally and intensely involved with the Word of God in order to develop worry-defeating faith. As Dr. David Gibbs of the Christian Law Association preaches, "You need to mega dose on the Word of God." Attend a church regularly where the Word is being ministered. Become aware of and watch television programs that feed your faith. Listen to the Word while you drive. Worship while washing dishes. Meditate while taking a bath. Be ceaseless

YOU MUST GET VERY PERSONALLY AND INTENSELY INVOLVED WITH THE WORD OF GOD IN ORDER TO DEVELOP WORRY-DEFEATING FAITH.

and relentless in seeking God. Make time every day to get alone with God and His Word. Sound fanatical? Perhaps but it works! Your faith needs the Word as much as your body needs food, maybe even more.

Why is it so important to constantly feed faith? Did you know every experience you have impacts your faith? The strength of your faith is either being boosted or drained by your daily activities. It is a matter of spiritual life or death that you take in more faith than you expend. Should part of exercising faith be to speak to the "mountain"? What mountain? A literal mountain? Yes, a properly fed and exercised faith could move a literal mountain. But, the emotional, financial, and physical mountains are also moveable. When worry-defeating faith operates within you, anything that causes doubt or anxiety can be removed.

Here is where Christians often miss the simple instructions of the Bible. What do we do to our mountains? We ask God to remove them. We ask other people to help us pray those mountains away. We say God put them there to teach us a lesson. Yet the Lord says, "say to this mountain" (Matthew 17:20). Simply speak directly to the thing causing the problem in your life.

Is what you say important? Sure it is! Consider the world of economics. How does talk affect the economy of nations? Suppose a group of people began to think and say times are going to get bad. What happens? Talk goes out… "Times are getting bad, times are getting bad." More and more people and business owners then talk that talk. They start to believe it. They hold back on spending and creating jobs because they heard times are getting bad. When spending and jobs are cut back, sure enough, times start to get bad. What follows are more cutbacks of individuals and businesses. The snowball is now set in motion, and times really get bad; thus, talk of economics serves as one cause for the slow down. The talk and rumor that "times are getting bad" turns out to be a self-fulfilling prophecy. This description of an economic slow-down is over simplified; however, even the expert will confirm "talk" is extremely important in terms of economic trends.

Consider the political arena. Question any political consulting firm, and you'll be told one of the first objectives in a major campaign is to "get the talk right." Get to the man on the street and get him to start making favorable comments about the candidate and campaign. Getting the talk right helps to create the public image that the campaign is moving along positively. If the talk is right, the public should start to perceive the candidate as a winner.

WHEN WORRY-DEFEATING FAITH OPERATES WITHIN YOU, ANYTHING THAT CAUSES DOUBT OR ANXIETY CAN BE REMOVED.

Most of us like to go with the winner, so that particular candidate will pick up many more votes because he is perceived as the winner. Why? Because the talk was right. While this example is oversimplified, it holds valuable truth.

Talk is important. Talk is no less important in the spiritual realm for removing mountains in your life. If for no other reason, talk is important because Jesus says it is.

What is your mountain? What is causing worry in your life? Speak to it in the name of Jesus and on the authority of God's Word. Speaking to the mountain may be a new concept to you, but it is vital and it does work. Say something like, "Mountain, I speak to you in faith because the Word of God tells me to do so. Jesus told me you had to obey. I am commanding you in Jesus' name to be cast down. You are no longer an obstacle for me. I am free from the worry you have caused me." Then thank God you are free and continue to confess regardless of what you see or how you feel.

From this point forward, when you bring this mountain before God, do so in an attitude of praise, telling Him you have accepted your deliverance. Remember: once you speak to the mountain, do not let any statement of unbelief come from your mouth again concerning that mountain. If you do, confess your doubt to God and resume your attitude of faith concerning that need. Do not misunderstand. Simply speaking something DOES NOT make it so. However, if Jesus said speaking to mountains is an IMPORTANT PART of having our needs met, then we better start speaking in order to receive His promise.

Even when Satan uses the spirit of fear to plant doubt in your mind, reject it by using the Word of God. And do not let that doubt pass through your lips. I like what the dynamic Bible teacher Charles Capps says, "Doubt will die unborn unless you speak it."

BELIEVING IN FAITH

The next faith building exercise is BELIEVING. Remember the instructions of Jesus in chapter 11 of the Gospel according to Mark? "For verily I say unto you, That whosoever shall say unto this mountain, Be thou removed and be thou cast into the sea; and shall not doubt in his heart…he shall have whatsoever he saith… whatever things so ever ye desire, when ye pray, believe that ye receive *them*, and ye shall have *them*" (Mark 11:22–24).

Again, to receive this promise you MUST speak and believe. To believe is to decide that regardless of what others tell you, what your body tells you, WHAT THE DEVIL tells you, or what your emotions tell you, you are going to stand on the Word of God with the knowledge in your spirit that the mountain will be removed.

> TO BELIEVE IS TO DECIDE THAT REGARDLESS OF WHAT OTHERS TELL YOU, WHAT YOUR BODY TELLS YOU, WHAT THE DEVIL TELLS YOU, OR WHAT YOUR EMOTIONS TELL YOU, YOU ARE GOING TO STAND ON THE WORD OF GOD

In Psalm 1:3 David does a magnificent job of describing the person who is exercising true belief in the Word of God: "He shall be like a tree planted by the rivers of water, that bringeth forth his fruit in his season; his leaf also shall not wither; and whatever he doeth shall prosper." Is that not great…an iron clad, airtight promise of prosperity to those who will obey God's Word?! But how did this man get to be like a "tree planted by the rivers of water"? How did he come to believe like that? Verses one and two of same chapter leave no doubt about the answer. His delight, or love, is the law of the Lord and he meditates on that.

CHAPTER 5

LOOK TO THE WORD

As you are aware by now, the Word of God is the Christian's source of strength. What magnificent praiseworthy work…the Word of GOD is! It is timeless and universal. Its impact will last an eternity. Yet it's so personal, speaking to individuals as if designed for each person exclusively.

Paul instructed Timothy to "Study to shew thyself approved unto God, a workman that needeth not be ashamed, rightly dividing the Word of truth" (II Timothy 2:15). In other words, Paul's message to Timothy and to us is to Study this Word of God and stay involved with it. Therefore, when you need it, you will know what it says and how it works. You will have no reason to be ashamed.

A closer look at Paul's admonition reveals he is saying be diligent with the Word of God. Stick to it! Stick with it! As you do, you will prove to yourself it works. You will become a teacher, an example who will never have to be timid about it.

It stands to reason then if the Word is not studied, the time will come when it is needed and shame will result. Hosea, inspired by God, best described this situation when he wrote, "My people are destroyed for a lack of knowledge..." (Hosea 4:6). If a lack of knowledge will cause one to be destroyed, then an abundance of knowledge will cause a person to prosper in every area of life. Remember: the Word of God has the answer to all possible situations that could bring worry into your life!

> REMEMBER: THE WORD OF GOD HAS THE ANSWER TO ALL POSSIBLE SITUATIONS THAT COULD BRING WORRY INTO YOUR LIFE!

A word study of the Scripture in Hosea reveals *destroyed* can be defined as "silenced" and *knowledge* means "cunning." In other words, the prophet declares God's people are silenced because they don't know what to do. Looking into the Word, the believers' fixed point of reference will instruct us in what to do!

The Word of God is the final authority on the earth. The final authority is not technology, which is in a state of constant flux. Great technological advancements are outdated and nearly obsolete by the first day they hit the market. The final authority is not medicine, which keeps men with great medical minds shaking their heads in puzzlement when dealing with a simple virus. The final authority on the earth is not political power, in which constant change in policy, direction, and players in the political arena is the name of the game.

Thank God for technological advances, medical discoveries, and Christian public servants who promote the liberties of our land. However, they are limited, and they do change. God and His Word are the only two constants. "Heaven and earth shall pass away, but my words shall not pass away" (Matthew 24:35).

It is impossible for the Word of God and fear to truly abide in the same area of your life. If fear is at work, causing worry, then in that particular situation you are not operating on the promises of God. Satan uses fear largely to promote, magnify, and make you anxious over the unknown. *How will the bills be paid? Will I be healed? Will I keep my job? Will my family stay together?*

As is true in the natural realm, the unknown generates fear in our personal lives. For example, you hear tapping on the window late at night. Fear strikes. Not a fear of sound, but a fear of the unknown. Upon looking out the window, you discover the wind has caused a branch from a nearby tree to hit the window. When the **source** of the sound is recognized, fear of the unknown is no longer a threat.

A child hesitates before entering a dark room. The darkness itself can do the child no harm. Because of the darkness, however, the child cannot see who or what is in the room. When the lights are turned on, and the child finds nothing harmful, he will enter the room. To remove the unknown is to remove the fear.

Get hold of this spiritual parallel: The Word of God is the KNOWN. It is eternal. It never changes. It will work for you personally because the Living Word, Jesus Christ, lives inside of you.

If the KNOWN abides in you then the fear of the unknown is never an insurmountable problem.

JESUS LIVES IN YOU!

Matthew refers to Jesus' residence in the believer as the Kingdom of God. Matthew records Jesus' thoughts concerning basic physical and material needs of life. He states emphatically the believer should not get disturbed over what he will eat, drink, or wear. Jesus delivered one of the most profound truths of His ministry when He proclaimed, "Seek ye first the kingdom of God, and his righteousness; and all these things shall be added unto you" (Matthew 6:33). We know "these things" refers to items needed for eating, drinking, and wearing. But where is the kingdom, and how do we obtain the righteousness of God?

The worried person often looks to "things" as the way out. If I had money…if my marriage was stable…if I were popular…if I had a job. Many people go through life saying, "If just this one thing was taken care of, I could relax." When that thing is over, however, it is then another thing, and another, and so on.

> GET HOLD OF THIS SPIRITUAL PARALLEL: THE WORD OF GOD IS THE KNOWN. IT IS ETERNAL. IT NEVER CHANGES. IT WILL WORK FOR YOU PERSONALLY BECAUSE THE LIVING WORD, JESUS CHRIST, LIVES INSIDE OF YOU.

Jesus says to forget "things." Seek the kingdom for the necessary and desired things are in the kingdom. Which kingdom…Heaven? No. Many people interpret the kingdom referenced here as Heaven and say, "Well, I'll have all the things I need when I get to Heaven." However, Jesus taught his disciples to pray to the Father, "Thy will be done on earth as it is in heaven" (Matthew 6:10). If it weren't God's desire for His will to be done in earth as it is in heaven, Jesus would not have taught His disciples to pray that way. No, the kingdom referenced was not Heaven. God does not want His children to wait until they get to Heaven to have their needs met. He wants them to have the abundant life now, here on the earth!

THE KINGDOM IS A SPIRITUAL ENTITY THAT IS ESTABLISHED INSIDE EVERY BORN AGAIN CHRISTIAN.

The kingdom referred to is a spiritual entity that is established inside every born again Christian. What did Jesus mean when He said seek the kingdom first and His righteousness and you will have everything else?

Jesus was saying:

1. **Realize that the kingdom of God is in you.** Someone said, "The kingdom is where the king is." Jesus, the King, is in your spirit. So is the kingdom. Simply stated, the kingdom will produce in you a life of God's way of doing and being.

2. **Continue to broaden your knowledge about the kingdom that is in you.**

3. Begin to operate in the principles of the kingdom.

There is enough power, authority, information and promises in the kingdom to solve all your problems. So seek the kingdom that can bring you victory in EVERY circumstance, not the "THING" that temporarily puts out one fire in your life. If you are studying God's Word and obeying the voice of the Holy Spirit, the Kingdom of God is growing in you every day.

For concern and doubt to consume you, they would have to conquer Jesus in you. That is not going to happen. So, Christian, why are you worried? Praise God you "are more than conquerors through him who loved us" (Romans 8:37).

In looking to the Word, the child of God can find many marvelous promises that speak to specific types of needs, desires, and situations. Here are some steps to aid the Winning Witness when relating to the Word:

1. Take the promises personally.

Psalm 16:5 says the King is the "portion of mine inheritance and of my cup: thou maintainest my lot." The Winning Witness knows God promises to belong to him personally and God will perform what He promises (Jeremiah 1:2).

2. Prepare your heart and mind to receive.

The Winning Witness knows the heart and mind must be in the condition to be good ground for the Word. The Winning Witness learns quickly that unconfessed sin must be brought to God. Psalm 66:18 says, "If I regard iniquity in my heart, the Lord will not hear me." The Winning Witness who is struggling in believing God to meet particular needs will be strengthened by Psalm 119:32: "I will run the way of thy commandments, when thou shalt enlarge my heart." The idea is when we receive this truth, God will enlarge our capacity to receive His promises.

3. Do your part.

The Winning Witness remembers God's promises are conditional. A *Bible fact* is a statement about God, regardless of whether we accept it or not. A *Bible promise* is a fact that requires action before it will work. In that light, the importance of the instruction of James 1:22 is magnified: "Be doers of the Word, and not hearers only, deceiving yourselves."

4. Wait for God's Method and God's Time.

The Winning Witness remembers that God knows the best way and time to meet our needs. Hebrews 6:12 offers a very important key to receiving the promises of

God. "That ye be not sluggish, but followers of them who through faith and patience inherit the promises." The chapters on exercising faith and patience are very important on your way to becoming a Winning Witness.

Are you worried about being inadequate to face life's challenges? Consider the following Scriptures:

Isaiah 45:24 "Surely shall one say, in the LORD have I righteousness and strength."

Psalms 37:4–5 "Delight thyself also in the LORD, and he shall give thee the desires of thine heart. Commit thy way unto the LORD; trust also in him; and he shall bring it to pass."

Psalms 1:3 "He shall be like a tree planted by the rivers of water, that bringeth forth his fruit in his season, his leaf also shall not wither; and whatsoever he doeth shall prosper."

Hebrews 4:16 "Let us therefore come boldly unto the throne of grace…and find grace and mercy to help in time of need.

Are you worried about guilt in your life? Now there's a tool with which the devil will whip you if you let him.

But the Bible says you are not guilty once you confess anything to the Lord. Explore these verses:

Romans 8:1 "There is therefore now no condemnation to them which are in Christ Jesus, who walk not after the flesh, but after the Spirit.

Romans 3:24 "Being justified freely by his grace though the redemption that is in Christ Jesus."

II Corinthians 5:21 "For he hath made him to be sin for us, who knew no sin; that we might be made the righteousness of God in him."

Isaiah 43:25 "I, even I, am he that blotteth out thy transgressions for mine own sake; and will not remember thy sins."

Are you worried about money? Many times we can turn everything else over to God, but it seems difficult to develop our faith enough to believe God where financial needs are concerned. Honor God with your money. Tithe and give offerings. In fact, unless you are a tither, you really haven't made Jesus Lord of your financial resources.

If you dare to trust Him with your tithes and offerings then all of His promises regarding financial blessings will apply to you. You will see a great change in your faith. And God will bless you. Get hold of these verses concerning God's involvement in your finances. Consider the following:

Psalms 37:3 "Trust in the Lord, and do good; so shall thou dwell in the land, and verily thou shall be fed."

Philippians 4:19 "But my God shall supply all your need according to his riches in glory by Christ Jesus."

Deuteronomy 29:9 "Keep therefore the words of this covenant, and do them, that ye may prosper in all that ye do."

Luke 12:28 "If then God so clothe the grass, which is today in the field, and tomorrow is cast into the oven; how much more will he clothe you, O ye of little faith?"

Matthew 7:11 "If ye then, being evil, know how to give good gifts to your children, how much more shall your Father which is in heaven give good things to them that ask him?"

Do doubts and fears give you a problem? This is another attempt by Satan to steal from you the abundant life Christ has given you. Use some of the following verses to conquer doubt and fear in your life:

Philippians 4:13 "I can do all things through Christ which strengtheneth me."

II Corinthians 3:5 "Not that we are sufficient of ourselves to think any thing as being of ourselves; but our sufficiency is of God."

Isaiah 41:10 "Fear thou not; for I am with thee: be not dismayed; for I am thy God. I will strengthen thee: yea, I will help thee; I will uphold thee with my righteousness."

Psalm 34:17 "The righteous cry, and the Lord heareth, and delivereth them out of all their troubles."

Psalms 112:7 "He shall not be afraid of evil tidings; his heart is fixed, trusting in the Lord."

So again, I ask you: Christian, what are you worried about? Whatever it is, the Word of God has the answer.

These quoted verses of Scripture do not come near to exposing even the tiniest tip of the iceberg of God's promises to us. **NOTE**…the more skillful and knowledgeable you become in God's Word, the less of a problem worry becomes. So continue to look to the Word, and worry will have no place in your life.

CHAPTER 6

ALWAYS
CAST YOUR CARE

The Christ follower has no business carrying any care. Contrary to much of what you are taught, see and believe that the child of God should be carefree! I Peter 5:7 spells it out clearly: "Casting **all** your care upon him; for he careth for you."

Do not misunderstand. Believers should take responsibility for their own spiritual development. They should bear one another's burdens in prayer before God. When a member of the body hurts, each individual should feel the impact. However, nowhere does the Bible say to continue to carry around care, yours or anyone else's. Instead, we are instructed to place them all on Jesus.

Why then was the picture of the beaten down, beggarly Christian historically presented regularly in sermons and songs in our churches? The Christian experience is not simply gaining access to Heaven because one went though hell on earth. Certainly, an eternity in Heaven is exciting beyond words, and surely there will be problems and needs on this earth. However, Jesus said all power had been given unto Him in ***earth*** (Matthew 28:18). You have the right to take His Name and His Word and use them where your needs are concerned.

YOU HAVE THE RIGHT TO TAKE HIS NAME AND HIS WORD AND USE THEM WHERE YOUR NEEDS ARE CONCERNED.

God does not want to withhold His blessings from you. God does not want you to wait until you get to Heaven to cast your care upon Him. He says, "Do it now!"

Songs and sermons that support the idea of Christians having little possibility of relief from trouble until they get to Heaven do an injustice to the Scriptures and to the child of God who needs help now. The Bible does not teach us to hang onto those cares until we arrive in Heaven and then lay them down. No, God wants our cares, all of them...now. In fact, the Greek word for "care," *merinama,* is also translated as *grief, concern, worry, oppression of the mind.* Anything in your life that falls into one of these categories, God says we are not to carry.

Why do Christians have the right to cast all care, grief, concern, worry and oppression of the mind onto Jesus? When you stop to think about it, this is a tremendous fringe benefit of being a child of God...an opportunity to be absolutely carefree! If it were possible to sell that privilege, most everyone you know would pay a great sum of money for the product, which would guarantee them, if they followed the directions properly, a life free of worry and care. This right is available to the Christian as part of his heritage.

THE BIBLE DOES NOT TEACH US TO HANG ONTO THOSE CARES UNTIL WE ARRIVE IN HEAVEN AND THEN LAY THEM DOWN. NO, GOD WANTS OUR CARES, ALL OF THEM...NOW.

Why is the casting of care possible? The Prophet Isaiah addresses this question: "Surely he hath borne our griefs and carried our sorrows: yet we did esteem him stricken, smitten of God, and afflicted. But he was wounded for our transgressions, he was bruised for our iniquities: the chastisement of our peace was upon him, and by his stripes we are healed" (Isaiah 53:4–5).

What a beautiful and total description Isaiah gives us of what Christ paid at Calvary. Jesus was your substitute. Whatever He endured at Calvary, you do not have to endure. **Jesus not only paid your sin debt, but also He took your sin as if He were you.** We have no trouble believing these verses of Scripture where our sins are concerned. We readily accept the fact He was wounded for our transgressions or sins, and He was bruised for our iniquity. We accept Him as our substitute in taking punishment for our sins. He also paid the price for our cares and worry. Yet most believers do not understand the work He did at the cross was for our spirit, soul and body!

MOST BELIEVERS DO NOT UNDERSTAND THE WORK HE DID AT THE CROSS WAS FOR OUR SPIRIT, SOUL AND BODY!

Human beings are, in reality, spirit beings. God is a spirit. We are made as spirit beings. We are eternal. We posses a soul (intellect, will, emotion). We live in a body temporarily, our "earth suit," if you will. By His death, burial and resurrection, Jesus did a work for all parts of our being…spirit, soul and body.

Many benefits of these verses are missed because we do not put all the promises into action. What else did Jesus do at Calvary? Look closely at those verses again. Jesus paid the price for our sickness. In addition, He served as our substitute for our griefs and sorrows. Is that to say that Jesus carried our griefs and sorrows at the same time He took our punishment for sins? Yes, that's exactly right!

You do not have to bear the pain and pressure of griefs and sorrows be-cause Jesus already did it

> YOU DO NOT HAVE TO BEAR THE PAIN AND PRESSURE OF GRIEFS AND SORROWS BECAUSE JESUS ALREADY DID IT FOR YOU.

for you. The same is true for our sickness and infirmities. The word *casting* in I Peter 5:7 indicates an on-going action is required.

While going through my difficulties in life, I found myself casting care every few minutes. Because worry can quickly build a stronghold, I learned to cast care in its embryo stage. Never let care hang around in your mind. As the weeks passed, my temptation to worry became less and less frequent. To this day, however, worry will raise its ugly head from time to time. The same God given right to cast care and win over worry works just as effectively now as it did 20 years ago when I started learning these principles.

We are instructed to cast care the same way we give Him our sins, by acting in faith on His Word. A good way to receive this promise is to say, "God, I believe Jesus was my substitute. Anything He took, I don't have to take. He took my griefs and sorrows. God, you know the care (worry) in my heart (or sickness in my body). I'm casting it on Jesus. He has done all the work necessary for my victory. The care is in His hands. Thank You that now Jesus is involved."

> WE ARE INSTRUCTED TO CAST CARE THE SAME WAY WE GIVE HIM OUR SINS, BY ACTING IN FAITH ON HIS WORD.

To some degree, it's a wasted effort on the part of Jesus when we don't take full advantage of everything He paid for at Calvary. If part of the purpose of His tremendous humiliation and great pain was to pay for our griefs and sorrows (worries), then we are not only hurting ourselves, but we are also doing a great disservice to the work of Jesus by continuing to carry our cares.

Generally, Christians encounter two problems when casting care:

1. We do not cast the care until we are at a crisis point.

2. We do not leave the care with Jesus.

Let us discuss both problems in detail. Often, when pressures and problems arise, we give little thought to following the instruction in I Peter 5:7 until our situation is out of control. The Bible does not say to use our own wisdom and resources to deal with a care until we reach the end of our rope and then cast it on Jesus. Most of the time, it's late in the game when we cast our care. Sometimes, we never cast some cares.

> THE BIBLE DOES NOT SAY TO USE OUR OWN WISDOM AND RESOURCES TO DEAL WITH A CARE UNTIL WE REACH THE END OF OUR ROPE AND THEN CAST IT ON JESUS.

Jesus wants them all. He wants them in their infant stages, though.

Abram, later called Abraham, was a great man of faith, but he sometimes had a problem giving a situation to God. In Genesis 12:7, God speaks to Abraham and tells him he has arrived at the place to be given to him and his seed. In other words, God said, "Abram, you are here. This is the place I promised you. You and future generations of your family shall occupy this land." After God spoke to Abram, famine came upon the land (Genesis 12:10). What did Abram do? Did he say, "Now, God, You said this is my land and no famine is going to move me"? Did he give God the situation and the care? No, he took matters into his own hands. He fled to Egypt, a biblical type of bondage. Sure, the care was handled, but it was handled with Abram's wisdom and resources. And what a price to pay! It was in Egypt where Abram obtained Hagar, the Egyptian maid. Abram later fathered a child by Hagar. Future generations of that offspring, Ishmael, brought war and hardship upon the children of Israel…a conflict that continues to this day.

Many of the critical challenges faced by the nation of Israel today can be traced to Ishmael and Isaac. It was in Egypt where Lot, who traveled with Abram, was exposed to the immoral lifestyle and lay of the land, which later attracted him to Sodom and Gomorrah because they looked like Egypt (Genesis 15:13).

The point is simply this: By not standing on the promise of God in the face of famine, by not giving his worry and care to God, Abram not only impaired his own progress, but also he planted the bad seed that adversely affected generations upon generations of the nation of Israel.

Consider the second problem of casting your care: leaving it with God. Once you make the decision to accept what Jesus did at Calvary, the devil will disturb your decision and steal your peace in the matter by using things that worry you.

WHEN YOU SAY TO GOD YOU ARE GIVING HIM THE CARE OF A PARTICULAR SITUATION FROM THIS POINT ON, THE DEVIL WILL SEND THE SPIRIT OF FEAR TO TRY AND OPERATE IN YOUR MIND.

When you say to God you are giving Him the care of a particular situation from this point on, the devil will send the spirit of fear to try and operate in your mind. You have a choice. You will stand firmly and say, "I don't accept your fear and worry. I've given the care of this problem to God." Otherwise, you allow fear and doubt to begin to function in your mind, and you, in effective, will pick up that care and start carrying it again.

God continues to honor our freedom of choice. If we choose to take back a care from Him, He will freely allow us to carry it again. If we start worrying again about a care we previously gave to Him, we are, in essence, saying to God, "I want it back." God will honor that request. As noted previously, it is necessary we understand God is a gentleman.

GOD CONTINUES TO HONOR OUR FREEDOM OF CHOICE. IF WE CHOOSE TO TAKE BACK A CARE FROM HIM, HE WILL FREELY ALLOW US TO CARRY IT AGAIN.

Notice the verse I Peter 5:6: "Humble yourself." In other words, bring yourself under the discipline and control of God. In this context, the road to humility is "casting your care." The opposite of humble is pride. Our attempts to navigate through a problem without "casting the care" is at its root a manifestation of pride. The Scriptures teach us "pride goes before a fall."

To avoid the fall, cast your care. Christ's supernatural work and strength is in you, therefore, separate the pressure from the problem.

A major part in becoming a worry-free Christian is learning to leave the care with God. How is this done? When the very first hint of doubt and fear enters your mind over the care you gave to God, stop instantly and deal with it. Do not allow ten minutes, ten hours, or ten days of worry to pass. Bind that spirit at once!

Then praise God for your deliverance, your victory, your healing, and your prosperity. Give Him

> A MAJOR PART IN BECOMING A WORRY-FREE CHRISTIAN IS LEARNING TO LEAVE THE CARE WITH GOD.

praise, even though you may not see or feel anything happen. Continue to praise God and believe His Word. Praise strengthens faith. Praise causes the devil to flee. Praise pleases God. Praise shows God your faith is operating, regardless of what your physical senses are telling you. The Bible says God **inhabits** the praises of His people (Psalms 22:3).

Praise is where God lives. As has been said, "Praise is God's address." Leaving your care with Jesus and continuing to give God praise in the midst of the problem are two acts of faith that will guarantee God's support. His system and His Word make you a winner every time.

So what have we learned about casting our care?

1. Christians will not be problem free, but God wants us to be carefree.

2. Being carefree is accomplished by giving the care or worry of every anxious situation to God.

3. Being carefree also involves **leaving** the problem with God once you have given it to Him. Bind the devil's spirit of fear in your life at the first instance you feel it begin to operate.

4. Being carefree means praising God for winning over problems, even when victory is not clearly in sight.

When you learn to cast your care, leave it with God, and praise God in the midst of your trials. Your worries will begin to melt! On occasion, God will work an outright miracle. Sometimes, He will give you an idea or a way out of your problem, which you never considered. Know this: He will always honor His Word, and you **will** see God deal with your specific need.

CHAPTER 7

"XERCISE" PATIENCE

EXERCISE PATIENCE

Bible-based patience is one of the least understood yet most powerful forces available to the believer through God. Our understanding of patience is miles apart from its actual meaning and practical use. We labor under the misconception that only if we are patient and take our beatings a little longer maybe Satan will go away and leave us alone. Patience is not becoming a doormat to the devil.

During my earlier mentioned business and personal problems, more than one well-meaning Christian commented, "Look at him. He's still under that load. Most people would have forsaken God by now, but not him. He's being patient."

Later, the Holy Spirit showed me I was not exercising patience, but taking a whipping I could have cut short. There is a world of difference in Godly patience and getting knocked around by Satan.

This chapter deals with four important questions concerning patience:

1. What is God kind patience?

2. Who has it?

3. How is it applied and exercised?

4. What are the results of exercising this kind of patience in our lives?

I recommend you read this chapter several times, especially if the meaning of power and patience is unclear to you. On the authority of God's Word, I can tell you that once you understand patience, how faith and patience work hand-in-hand, and how to fully applying this important power to your life will you be well on your way to winning over worry. Ask God now, before you read any further, to open the eyes of your understanding. Believe that His wisdom is operating in you. Tell Him you want to be fertile ground for His Word. Do it now, and you will recognize your insight broadening and your life changing as this power grows in you.

Luke 21:19 states, "In your patience possess ye your souls."

EXERCISE GODLY PATIENCE

What is Godly kind patience? Patience, like faith, is a force. It is a power. It is a grace given by God. It is not a frame of mind. It is not an attitude. It is not desperately clinging to Christianity in the hope that if you hang on long enough, you will make it into Heaven with Satan breathing down your neck. There is liberty in patience. When your faith is exercised in believing God for a need to be met, patience will support your faith and allow it to continue to work.

> PATIENCE, LIKE FAITH, IS A FORCE. IT IS A POWER. IT IS A GRACE GIVEN BY GOD. IT IS NOT A FRAME OF MIND. IT IS NOT AN ATTITUDE.

Who has patience? Paul writes in the Book of Galatians that patience (or long-suffering) is part of the fruit of the Spirit: "But the fruit of the Spirit is love, joy, peace, longsuffering, gentleness, goodness, faith, meekness, temperance: against such there is no law" (Galatians 5:22–23).

In other words, just like all other graces in the fruit of the Spirit, God has given all believers patience. So asking God for patience is not a correct prayer request. Christians already have patience. Our prayers should be that God help us to apply and increase the patience we possess.

How is patience exercised? Patience, like faith, needs to be fed the Word of God. The first step in exercising patience is to learn all you can about this power in your life. Consider what patience does for you in defeating worry. James gives us a dynamic picture of what patience accomplishes in the lives of those who practice it. He writes, "My brethren, count it all joy when ye fall into divers temptations; knowing this, that the trying of your faith worketh patience. But let patience have her perfect work, that ye may be perfect and entire, wanting nothing" (James 1:2–4).

> HOW IS PATIENCE EXERCISED? PATIENCE, LIKE FAITH, NEEDS TO BE FED THE WORD OF GOD. THE FIRST STEP IN EXERCISING PATIENCE IS TO LEARN ALL YOU CAN ABOUT THIS POWER IN YOUR LIFE.

James' statement "count it all joy" during tests and trails makes more sense when we understand the trial is a vital ingredient in developing our patience. Paul makes the same comment to the church in Rome: " …but we glory in tribulations also, knowing that tribulation worketh patience" (Romans 5:3). Properly handled, tribulations (trials, tests and temptations) in the end can cause patience to grow stronger in us. It is ironic that the very experience designed to hamper our growth and destroy us is the same action that puts patience to work and causes us to arrive at a place of being perfect, complete, entire and wanting nothing!

IT IS NECESSARY TO UNDERSTAND THAT PATIENCE DOES NOT REALLY GO TO WORK UNTIL THE TRIAL OR WORRY COMES.

It is necessary to understand that patience does not really go to work until the trial or worry comes. However, as it works in you, patience becomes stronger, much like a muscle in your body. The more patience works, the stronger it gets. The stronger it gets, the more it works. Therefore, the temptation or tribulation sent to try your faith only serves to develop your patience.

We can begin to understand why our faith needs our patience when tests and trials come. Underdeveloped patience leaves our faith exposed to the doubt and fear of Satan. Also understand patience won't come if we don't choose to exercise it. When the temptations mentioned by James come to try your faith, you can put patience to work, or you can panic, worry, and let the spirit of fear control you. God will not force patience on you. It is your choice to exercise it.

DEVELOP RESULTS

What are the results of exercising patience? Godly patience, properly exercised and developed, will do much to set you free from worry. To understand the result of using it, however, we must understand how true patience works through us.

PATIENCE DOES ITS BEST WORK FROM THE TIME A PROBLEM IS PUT IN GOD'S HANDS UNTIL THE SITUATION IS RESOLVED...

Patience, by definition, is constant. Consider the spiritual application of patience and what it looks like in a person while in use. You have a need. Something is causing you worry and concern. You exercise your faith. You believe in your heart and confess with your mouth. At this point, properly developed patience is your best friend. It is at that moment you call on your patience to assist your faith. Your patience should operate fully from the time you believe God has met a need until the time you see an outward manifestation that your problem is solved.

Patience does its best work from the time a problem is put in God's hands until the situation is resolved…in other words, the interim period when there is no outward sign the need is being met. It may be three minutes, three weeks or three years. Patience is a supernatural helpmate to our faith.

> IF PATIENCE IS AT WORK, YOU WILL BEHAVE, BELIEVE, ACT AND SPEAK AS IF YOU HAVE ALREADY SEEN YOUR NEED MET OR PROBLEM SOLVED.

Patience in action will cause you to act the same or be constant while you are trusting God. If patience is at work, you will behave, believe, act and speak as if you have already seen your need met or problem solved. You will know your faith was released. You will have an expectant attitude. Properly developed patience causes you to come through any test or trial without being controlled by doubt and fear.

Can you see why patience is such an important partner to faith? Worry consumes faith and causes our minds to faint. If patience is at work, it allows faith to do its job without being affected by worry. Consider more of what the Bible says about constancy and expectancy. In the Book of Hebrews, Christians are to "run with patience the race that is set before us, looking unto Jesus, the author and finisher of our faith" (Hebrews 12:1–2). In other words, run the race of a Christian life the same way all the time. Run when you don't feel like it. Run when Satan tries to tell you times are bad. Be constant in your running.

IF PATIENCE IS AT WORK, IT ALLOWS FAITH TO DO ITS JOB WITHOUT BEING AFFECTED BY WORRY.

To run with patience is to run expecting to win. Regardless how steep the incline, expect to go over the top. Regardless how complicated the problem, expect it to be resolved. At the crest of the hill and in the middle of the crisis, know this: You have won by "looking unto Jesus, the author and finisher of your faith" (Hebrews 12:2). Jesus is a winner. He won over everything Satan could throw at Him, including hell itself.

As discussed earlier, Jesus is in you! If He reigns in your spirit, then you are a winner, too! By expecting to win and being constant in your actions and speech in the face of trials, you are exercising your God given patience and your faith is strengthened. Do you want to make yourself a legitimate candidate for the promises of God? The anointed writer of the Book of Hebrews tells you how to do it: "That you do not become sluggish, but imitate **those** who through **faith** and **patience** inherit the promises" (Hebrews 6:12). Is that to say if the faith and patience God gives us are developed enough, then all the promises of God can be ours? Certainly! If **"those"** can inherit the promises of God through faith and patience, then you can, too. God is no respecter of persons; He has no prejudice or special treatment of anyone.

One other thing about patience…just because you decide to be constant while believing God to meet a need does not mean those around you

JUST BECAUSE YOU DECIDE TO BE CONSTANT WHILE BELIEVING GOD TO MEET A NEED DOES NOT MEAN THOSE AROUND YOU WILL MAKE THE SAME DECISION.

will make the same decision. Your closest friend, next-door neighbor, brother, or even spouse can be your biggest obstacle in continuing to trust God without wavering. For example, suppose you have a need and have turned it over to God. You released your faith, and your patience is at work. Along comes someone very close to you. Perhaps that person also has a vital interest in that need. The question is posed to you, "What are you going to do?" You answer, "I'm believing God. I have put the care in His hands. I asked for His wisdom in what to do. As far as I am concerned, the problem is solved."

Here is where the situation can be sticky. If the other person is not operating in patience, his response might be something like, "Well, believing God is fine, but if the problem is solved, why can't we see the results? You're not being realistic. It seems to me you should show some concern."

REMEMBER: THE TOUGHER THE TEST, THE HARDER YOUR PATIENCE WILL WORK—IF YOU LET IT. THE CORRECT RESPONSE HERE SHOULD BE ONE OF LOVE, NOT AN ANGRY REBUTTAL.

The tendency here of many believers is to start to come unglued. No doubt, Satan has already tried to bring pressure on you about the need. Now here is someone close to you saying you are not being realistic, and you apparently do not care. The trial is intensified. Whether the other person knows it or not, Satan will attempt to use him or her to get to you.

Remember: the tougher the test, the harder your patience will work—if you let it. The correct response here should be one of love, not an angry rebuttal. You might reply with something like, "I know this is important to you. It is important to me, too. That is why I put it in God's hands. I know He is committed, and He will provide the answer if I believe."

Let us recap the important points concerning patience and how it helps us overcome worry:

1. Patience is a force or power, not an attitude.

2. God has given patience to every born again person. Developing and using patience is a choice of every individual.

3. When in operation, patience will cause a person to be steady and stable, rather than be worried while believing God will meet a particular need.

4. Tests, trials and temptations put patience to work; thus, patience grows stronger.

5. Patience is a helpmate to faith. Patience should be of special assistance from the time a situation is given to God until there is an outward sign the need is met.

Praise God, you are now equipped with everything you need to be a "winning warrior." Now, it's just a matter of learning how to use all that God has made available. Faith and patience, properly utilized, will open God's storehouse of promises. Both forces reside inside the Christian. You have the potential inside you to overcome anything that will cause you anxiety or stress. Feed the forces of faith and patience with the Word of God, so you can **know the truth**, and you can be set free!

FAITH AND PATIENCE, PROPERLY UTILIZED, WILL OPEN GOD'S STOREHOUSE OF PROMISES. BOTH FORCES RESIDE INSIDE THE CHRISTIAN.

CHAPTER 8

NOW RELAX

A s a new person in Christ, God has made you all sufficient. Everything you need to defeat worry is either in you or available to you though God's Word. Only knowledge and skill separate you from a life free from worry. Not a life free of problems, but free from the care of those problems. Liberty-producing knowledge, of course, comes from God and His instructions for our lives. The true overcomer, the worry-free individual, must be exposed consistently and intensely to God's Word through conversations with teachers, preachers, Bible study groups and in individual prayer and study, songs and other legitimate methods. If necessary, rearrange some of your priorities, go to bed later, get up earlier, watch less TV, turn off the computer, or do whatever it takes to get fed regularly and nutritiously from God and His Word.

Realize the promises and tools God has made available to you are of little practical use if you don't know they exist or how to use them. Just as faith "cometh by hearing, and hearing by the word of God" (Romans 10:17), skill in using God's Word comes with practice in applying the Word.

To become skillful at almost anything, whether your professional career, your golf game or your role as a partner, requires practice. Yet, in the spiritual realms, we do not practice. Has this ever been true in your life? You discover a spiritual truth or promise in God's Word. The next step is to "try it on for size." You may try to use it once or twice. If you see no immediate noticeable results, then you simply cast it aside saying to yourself, "Well, it didn't work for me; I guess it's just not for everyone; I guess if God wants me to have that blessing, He will just drop it on me." Or "God is just holding that back from me to teach me a lesson."

> REALIZE THE PROMISES AND TOOLS GOD HAS MADE AVAILABLE TO YOU ARE OF LITTLE PRACTICAL USE IF YOU DON'T KNOW THEY EXIST OR HOW TO USE THEM.

Know this: If God gives us a promise even once only in His Word, then it is true and unfailing for eternity. Furthermore, it is true for all who believe. The deficiency is not in God's Word, but in our skill in using it. Developing our spiritual skills takes practice, growth and maturity. Some of the principles discussed in this book may already be at work in your life. Others will probably come in a few weeks. Some may take months, and a few may take years for you to develop. However, that does not mean they are not true. They are just growing in your life as you practice them. Effective practice is not doing the wrong thing again and again. Some people say they have thirty years' experience as a Christian, when actually they've had one year's experience thirty times.

CONTRARY TO POPULAR BELIEF, PRACTICE DOES NOT MAKE PERFECT. EFFECTIVE PRACTICE IS NOT DOING THE WRONG THING AGAIN AND AGAIN.

Contrary to popular belief, practice does not make perfect. I once heard a football coach phrase it much better when he said, "Perfect practice makes perfect." All of your spiritual practice sessions will not be perfect, but stay in the Word and continue to strive for perfect practice in defeating worry. The devil will try to discourage you. Remember: the same Jesus who lives in you, defeated him. Satan is no match for the power in you.

Your well-meaning friends and close acquaintances will not always understand as you continue to grow toward a worry-free life. Remember: they have accepted excessive stress as normal living. Love them, but do not let them move you from your solid position in the Word of God. Just watch, gradually, some will come around to your way of thinking, believing and living. So RELAX!

> REMEMBER: THE SAME JESUS WHO LIVES IN YOU, DEFEATED HIM. SATAN IS NO MATCH FOR THE POWER IN YOU.

R – REALIZE THE EFFECT OF WORRY

Worry is a sin. Worry displeases God. Worry must be confessed before God. Worry never accomplished anything good.

E – EXERCISE FAITH

God has given you a measure of faith. His kind of faith. Faith feeds on the Word of God. Exercise your faith by believing in your heart, without doubting, and confessing with your mouth, that you will receive from God. As faith is exercised, it will believe in bigger and bigger things from God.

L – LOOK TO THE WORD

The Word of God is the source of faith and power. There is no lacking to the child of God who knows how to use the Word. There is nothing that you have ever worried about, are worried about, or that Satan tempts you to worry about that is not answered in the Word of God.

A – ALWAYS CAST YOUR CARE

Jesus took your griefs, sorrows, cares and depression at Calvary. He bore them. You are instructed to "cast all your care upon him, for he careth for you" (I Peter 5:7). Leave them there. Do not ask God to help you carry a burden when He wants you to thank Jesus for carrying it all.

X – "XERCISE" PATIENCE

The God given power of patience goes to work in the life of a Christian when tests and trials come. When exercised, patience will generate steadiness and stability in the midst of needs and problems. Patience will help the believer act, speak and believe in his heart that his needs have been met.

AND FURTHERMORE

"And furthermore" is a phrase my mother, who is with the Lord now, would repeat to me as a way of putting the bow on the proverbial package she had already verbally boxed and wrapped. "And furthermore" meant "here is just a little more food for thought." Experience has taught me some practical day-to-day strategies and methods of dealing with stress and anxiety.

YOU NEED TO BE GRATEFUL

Harlerin Hilton Hill is an outstanding host of a morning radio talk show in Knoxville, Tennessee. His opening remarks always include the following: "Welcome to this brand new day. This day has never been lived before. It is a blank canvas. If you will, it can be your masterpiece. As you wake up this morning, think of three things for which you are grateful. Gratitude makes all the difference in the world. Then go out and live this day with all the enthusiasm you can muster."

Gratitude...focus on what you have, not what you may have lost. Experts have determined that the subconscious mind accepts what you say, whether good or bad, as fact. Your mind then begins to work to bring your words into being. The Scriptures teach us to "Be careful for nothing; but in every thing by prayer and supplication, **with thanksgiving** let your requests be made known unto God. And the peace of God, which passeth all understanding, shall keep your hearts and minds through Christ Jesus" (Philippians 4:6–7). Always be on the look out for ways to express your gratitude.

YOU NEED TO SING

Dr. Clarence Sexton, founder and President of The Crown College in Knoxville, Tennessee, related an episode in his life and ministry. The pastor's day was not going as he desired. As a result, he became frustrated, disturbed and perhaps more than just a little grumpy. His wife and valuable helpmate, Evelyn, picked up on his mood. "Clarence," she exclaimed in no uncertain terms, "you need to sing." Friends, we need to sing. Singing is a stress repellant.

> "TRUST AND OBEY FOR THERE'S NO OTHER WAY TO BE HAPPY IN JESUS THAN TO TRUST AND OBEY."

I was driving to a business meeting on a Friday afternoon in a big city, battling rush hour traffic. I was uncertain about the exact location of the meeting and had no GPS. To make matters worse, it was raining (and I mean cats and dogs). One person in particular had driven more than two hours to attend the meeting. At best, it seemed I would be terribly late. At worst, I would not make it at all. Tension and anxiety started to become my close companions.

Out of the blue (literally), I recalled Mrs. Sexton's advice to her husband. I heard myself starting to sing that classic hymn *Trust and Obey.* "Trust and obey for there's no other way to be happy in Jesus than to trust and obey." As I sang, the tension lessened and anxiety dissipated. As peace began to infiltrate my mind, I was able to relax and focus. I made it to the meeting on time. The outcome was good.

Now I don't hold myself out to be an accomplished vocalist by any stretch of the imagination; however, my noise was as Psalm 100 instructs, "Joyful and unto the Lord." The moral of the story is when anxiety attacks, perhaps you need to sing.

A PERSONAL NOTE

THE GOAL IS GOD

Dr. Clarence Sexton was my pastor at Temple Baptist Church, Knoxville, Tennessee, while I was in graduate school. I sat under his ministry for less than four short years, but what an influence he continues to have on my life. I once heard him say, "Don't make a goal out of a by-product."

In God's work we learn about many wonderful "by-products." We are beneficiaries of God's love. We are undeserving recipients of His mercy. We are empowered by God's grace. We have a measure of God's faith. We are blessed with His miracles. And the list goes on.

> WE ARE EMPOWERED BY GOD'S GRACE. WE HAVE A MEASURE OF GOD'S FAITH. WE ARE BLESSED WITH HIS MIRACLES.

All these attributes and actions play a significant role in the life of the Christ follower…they matter…a lot. However, they are all "by-products" of our relationship with God. The goal should be God. "For in him we live, and move, and have our being…" (Acts 17:28).

OUR GOAL SHOULD BE GROWING OUR RELATIONSHIP WITH GOD. OUR GOAL SHOULD BE GETTING TO KNOW HIM BETTER THROUGH HIS WORD.

Our goal should be growing our relationship with God. Our goal should be getting to know Him better through His Word. After all, the Bible is about God, though wee meet other compelling figures like Noah, Abraham, Jonah, David, Isaiah, Peter, Paul and John. The Bible's sixty-six books, written by about 40 authors and inspired by the Holy Spirit, holds everything God wants us to know about Him.

Jesus teaches us to "seek ye first the kingdom of God and his righteousness; and all these 'things' shall be added unto you" (Matthew 6:33). Get to know God, and you will learn about the "things." They not only include the material, the physical and the financial area of our lives but also the promised by-products like love, joy, peace, hope, fulfillment and purpose.

REMEMBER THE GOAL IS GOD

G. Allen Jackson, pastor of World Outreach Church, Murfreesboro, Tennessee, penned it accurately in his book *Freedom From Worry* when he wrote, "The root of worry is fear. Trust is the antidote. The great challenge of our lives is to learn increment by increment to trust Him (God) implicitly, down to the finer points of daily living. Then we can begin to find victory over the worried mind." In those moments when we can't see God's hand, we learn to trust His heart.

> THE GREAT CHALLENGE OF OUR LIVES IS TO LEARN INCREMENT BY INCREMENT TO TRUST HIM (GOD) IMPLICITLY, DOWN TO THE FINER POINTS OF DAILY LIVING.

Congratulations on your decision to defeat worry in your life. Knowing and consistently acting upon the instructions of God's Word will guarantee your success.

To God Be The Glory!

NUGGETS

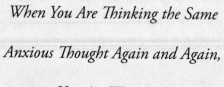

When You Are Thinking the Same

Anxious Thought Again and Again,

You Are Worrying.

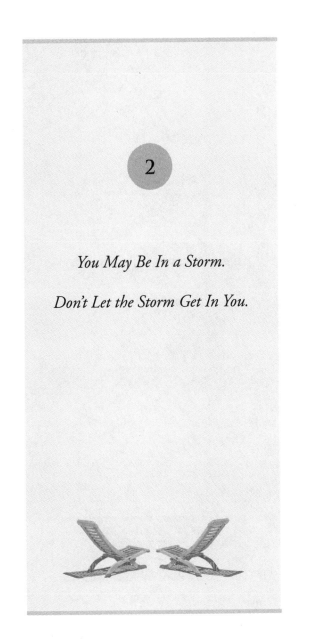

2

You May Be In a Storm.

Don't Let the Storm Get In You.

3

Don't React to Circumstances.

Respond to God.

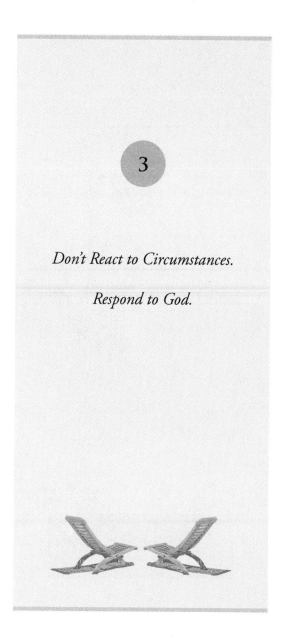

4

When The Holy Spirit Leads,

There May Be Urgency—

But There's No Anxiety.

5

Faith Does Not Deny Reality—

Faith Changes It.

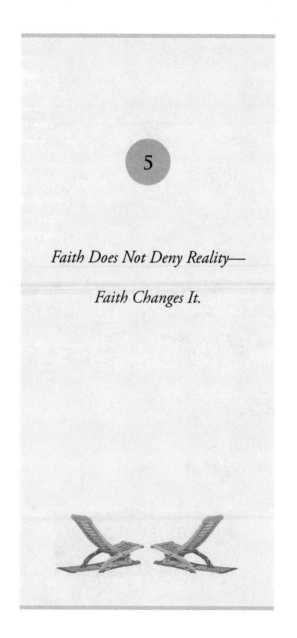

6

Your Future Is as Bright as

The Promise of God.

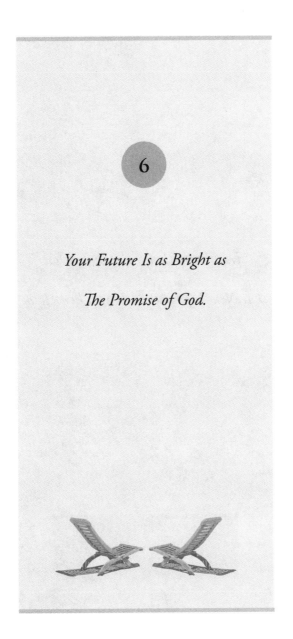

7

Transformation Is the Indication

that New Information Has Taken Hold.

ABOUT THE AUTHOR

Dwight Henry is an active and energetic man of many gifts. A city councilman, radio personality, hospice chaplain as well as former mayor, Tennessee State Representative, and gubernatorial candidate, Henry does not let much slow him down.

However, that was not the case some years ago when worry, anxiety and stress stopped him dead cold in his tracks.

Isolated in his home and seriously depressed in bed, a fateful walk to the kitchen for a glass of water one morning put him on a journey that would change his life forever.

If worry and the pressures of life rob you of hope and health, the God-inspired plan that Henry put into practice will produce for you the same results. Guaranteed!

Within two-and-a-half years of freeing himself from crippling isolation, Henry was elected mayor of his city. He credits his success to what he calls "The Relax Factor," a Bible-based, freedom-producing, supernaturally charged spiritual ingredient that produced a worry-free life—well, in the least, a life in which worry can be conquered in its very early stages.

Dwight Henry is delighted to believe with you, so you too can experience the same life-changing results. Be blessed and enjoy ***The Relax Factor:*** *Five Open Secrets to Winning Over Worry.*

To learn more about booking Dwight Henry to speak at your next event and for more inspirational "nuggets" connect with Dwight at www.DwightHenry.org.